D0858644

Amber
A VERY PERSONAL CAT

By Gladys Taber

Amber—A Very Personal Cat
Stillmeadow Album (*Photographs by Jacques Chepard*)
Especially Dogs—Especially At Stillmeadow
Stillmeadow Calendar
One Dozen And One
Gladys Taber's Stillmeadow Cook Book
Another Path
The Stillmeadow Road
Stillmeadow Sampler
Stillmeadow Day Book

Amber

A VERY PERSONAL CAT

by Gladys Taber

PARNASSUS IMPRINTS
Orleans, Massachusetts

For Kim Schneider
A rock and refuge—

Holly
Amber
Gladys Taber

Amber
A VERY PERSONAL CAT

Her amber eyes
Regard me steadfastly
With the grave wisdom of long ages past.
I am bewildered by their mystery
Too infinite to realize.

But suddenly I find I hold a kitten here,
Purring a love song in my ear.

Chapter 1

It was a cold November day and the sugar maples along the winding road to Stillmeadow stood bare against a pale sky. The air smelled of snow. I was coming home from Cape Cod to Connecticut with three friends, Helen, Vicky, and Margaret, but the little white farmhouse built in 1690 for once had no welcome. It was empty and so was the car. For the first time in fifteen years no Irish setter took up the whole back seat. My beloved champion Holly was not coming home again.

There seemed to be a loud stillness in the house as we stacked the luggage in the back kitchen beside the dog leashes, feeding pans, extra collars, combs and brushes. Nobody had a word to say.

Then I heard another car drive up, and I opened the back door (nobody ever uses the front door at Stillmeadow). I saw my daughter Connie climb out of the car and lift up an oblong black-handled case. When she came in, she put it down beside me and carefully unhooked the clasps and raised the cover.

A small triangular-shaped face set with a pair of topaz

eyes poked out, and after it came about eight ounces of kitten.

I almost never cry, but I burst into tears and simply sobbed while the morsel hopped in my lap and began to purr.

"It's an Abyssinian," I managed to say finally as the kitten kneaded my arms.

Now when my Siamese, Esmé, used to make the trip from New York to Stillmeadow and we opened the carrying case, she always uttered an ear-splitting screech, sped upstairs and hid behind the bathroom pipes. She usually stayed there three or four days, with room service up the steep ancient stairs. Tigger, our Manx, was raised in the country, and only once underwent the trip in the car to the veterinarian. His screams stopped a good many cars on the road as drivers craned their necks.

And when Aladdin, my first Abyssinian, came from Hollywood, he traveled in the Super Chief in a compartment with Smiley Burnette's wife. No carrying case for him to worry about. He slept in a basket lined with pink satin and had special meals cooked for him by an anxious chef.

Normally a cat takes some time to adjust to change, and I understand this very well since I hate change myself. But this new kitten was taking over socially from the first moment, and as soon as I stopped crying, she indicated that she was hungry and skipped ahead to the kitchen.

Connie unloaded her equipment. This included an aquamarine bathroom with plastic liners, a scoop for cleaning, two bags of sterilized kitty litter, a scratching

Aladdin, my first Abyssinian, came from Hollywood.

post covered with green wool carpet and topped with a catnip mouse on a coil, cans of special catfood, a bottle of vitamins, an envelope of instructions about diet, a bag of toys, and a folder of papers so that I could register her properly as the offspring of champions.

"We knew the house would be empty," Connie said as she put up the scratching post in the middle of my bedroom, "but Curtis and I felt you shouldn't be alone."

Abyssinians are rather rare and Connie and Curt had quite a time locating one. They finally found mine in, of all places, Staten Island.

This kitten had kept quiet all the way from Staten Island to Southbury, Connecticut.

I am not disparaging the Siamese or Manx, for any cat lover should have at least one of each. The Siamese is charming, passionate, uninhibited, beautiful. The Manx is steady, sensible as a banker, and the best mouser possible. Tigger reserved his deepest emotions for Esmé and kept bringing her mice and moles and laying them worshipfully at her paws. She never gave them a look.

Esmé was a one-person cat and I was the person. When I went away on a business trip, she would not speak to me when I got back. This might last two or three days. At the end of the time, she would stand on my desk and deliver a scorching indictment of people who left their cat. Then she forgave me in a dramatic scene worthy of Duse.

"I've brought everything," said Connie now, "so you won't need to let her out." She laid a small harness, collar and leash in my lap. "You wouldn't let her out in the snowdrifts anyway," she observed.

She was tactfully referring to Aladdin, that first Abyssinian, who went out one summer day when he was eight months old and was never seen again. Half the county turned out to hunt for him, and the loss was advertised on radio and in newspapers. We finally felt that someone had opened a car door to look at this unusual cat and sociable Aladdin hopped in and they went off. Aladdin never had a sense of direction; earlier he had got himself to the top of a 150-foot maple and did not know the way down. Our farmer neighbor, Frank, went up the tree and saved him while I stood dizzily below expecting them both to crash to death.

"Don't worry," said Frank, handing Aladdin over, "someone up there is looking after me." He pointed to the sky and smiled.

Naming the new kitten was quite a project. It was, in a way, just a matter of registering her, for I began calling her Sweetheart at once. Connie pointed out this would not look well on the papers although some of her champion ancestors had odd names, one called Eric and one Penny.

Of course she came to me when she felt like it, called or uncalled, and she felt like it so constantly that she might have been named Adhesive. Even now I often have to forego the can of French fried potatoes on the cellarway shelves because I cannot get the door ajar without having a golden shadow disappear into the catacombs of the cellar.

The first time I sat down to type, a small wedge-shaped head kept popping over the machine just in case an unwary key came up for her to catch. When I opened the drawer for manuscript paper, she vanished into the back of the drawer and settled into a four-inch

13

space while I wondered whether getting her out would ever be possible.

Still, she did need some sort of official name. When you decide to name an Abyssinian, the unusual apricot color seems important, and so does the history. Faith Baldwin suggested some Egyptian and Oriental names which were fascinating but which we finally decided were too imposing for such a small morsel. I liked Topaz, and Connie thought Buttercup would be good. But neither of these made good call names. My son-in-law settled it with Amber, which is euphonious and easy to say and fits the color.

Now the Abyssinian is supposed to be The Cat the Egyptians worshiped in the days of the pyramids. She was the cat goddess. From 3500 B.C. to 1970 is quite a span to retain a likeness, but Amber looks like some bas-reliefs I have seen of the Egyptian cat. The Abby has what experts call an oriental bone structure similar to the Siamese and is a small graceful slender cat with a coat difficult to describe. The undercoat and the delicate ears are apricot. The face is apricot with some darker overlay at the top, the eyes are golden or topaz and the nose itself is a small triangle of pinky brick. The whiskers are silvery with charcoal roots. The top coat has three different colors on each hair, and my own Amber has no intention of having me pull out a couple to put under a microscope in order to check whether the tip color is black or seal brown. The whole effect is luminous.

The tail is long and tapering, dark on the upper side and apricot on the under. The ears are sharply pointed triangles so delicate you can see light through them. The

Amber and I.

face below is another triangle, as is the jawline. The paw pads are charcoal.

It is no wonder the Egyptians felt this cat was a goddess!

Sometimes the Abyssinian is called the water cat, for according to one legend it was used as a fishing cat. What this means today is that I never turn on the hot water without being sure Amber is not in the sink. She spends a good deal of time in the shower too, just hoping a few drops will come down. There often is a trickle as well as some water on the stall itself, since the drain is not too reliable. She also likes to sit under the bathtub faucets to catch a drop or two.

I do not know whether other breeds ever love water so much. But Amber empties her own water dish daily and often takes a sip from my glass at breakfast time.

I always keep a glass of water on my bedside table, and the other night around midnight I heard a faint sound and turned the light on. Amber lifted her head from the glass and then dipped in and sipped earnestly. She drank a third of that water and then leaped to the bed and scrubbed her face before curling up to go to sleep again. I told her sleepily that we always provided room service at Stillmeadow.

Perhaps related to this love of water is her fanaticism for cleanliness. Like most cats, she washes herself constantly, polishing and repolishing, folding her ears flat with the impact of her paws and angling her hind legs out to scrub them thoroughly. But she also likes to be brushed four or five times a day, purring and kneading her paws as the brush goes over. And soon afterward she is washing her paws again. Being a short-hair she does not lose much hair, but she likes the feeling of being groomed.

One special characteristic of the Abyssinian, which may go back to the mysterious age of the pyramids, is the tone of voice. The miaow is so faint and deprecatory that it is hard to hear. I never had this trouble with the Siamese or the Manx. I began to wonder at first whether Amber could miaow. But when I took her to Dr. George Whitney in New Haven for a check up, she got bored in Ansonia and uttered a single lutelike cry and thrust both forelegs out of the breathing holes in the carrying case.

But the moment the case was open in the treatment room she began to purr. Then, instead of hiding behind the waste container, she leaped lightly to the cabinet and started taking caps from the medicine bottles. From there a swift leap took her to the high window ledge, where she could watch the dogs in the yard outside. When Dr. George came in, she greeted him happily and only uttered a delicate miaow as he gave her an enteritis injection. Afterward she sat on the table and scrubbed the disinfected area and purred again.

Buying a pedigreed cat is not always easy. Occasionally ads appear in a local newspaper when someone has a litter of Blue Point Siamese or of Persians, and some telephone books have listings. The directory of my nearest large city, however, only lists kennels. If you write The Cat Fanciers' Association, Inc., 20615 Patton Court, Detroit, Michigan, you will be able to get the names of breeders. Also *Cats' Magazine*, 2900 Jefferson Avenue, Washington, Pennsylvania, in every issue advertises cats and kittens of various breeds.

If there is a cat show in your area, this is an excellent

way to study the cats. Then you can choose the particular type of personality that fits yours best.

The Abyssinian, a rare breed, is expensive. Also the litters are small; two or three kittens is the usual number. Still, considering the Abby's charm, stability and loving disposition, I am sure the number available will increase markedly.

Once you have your pedigreed kitten, you register him or her as you register a pedigreed puppy. Even if you do not plan to have litters or go to cat shows, it is a good idea to have the registration, just as it is to have a school diploma!

There are various other ways to acquire a cat. In the country where I live, kittens bloom like the flowers in spring. One of the few free things in this expensive world is a kitten. Neighbors call one another up and suggest that they have the darlingest new batch of kittens. People run ads in the country newspaper. Notices on brown paper are posted regularly on trees or in store windows.

Or you can adopt a cat who is already in your yard. As I write, three cats are sitting by the well house, a smoky gray, a light orange, and a striped cat with white paws. They are thrifty, plump and able to fend for themselves. They are what we call barn cats and earn their shelter by keeping the rats from nearby barns. They are shy, but any of them would come in before long if I left the door ajar and in a week or two would be running the house.

Chapter 2

Cat nature has been speculated about for probably 4000 years, since the Egyptians first began to deify them. One thing is certain, the Egyptians used a cat head on the body of a woman for the goddess Bastet, who was the divinity of femininity and motherhood. Cats were mummified when they died, and anyone who killed a cat was likely to be put to death. Possibly this had a basis in economic necessity, for some authorities believe that only because the Phoenicians brought cats into Egypt was Egypt's grain saved.

When an Egyptian cat died, the man of the family is said to have shaved his eyebrows.

The Egyptians had a corner on cats until the Greeks began to steal them when most of the Greek granaries were being depleted by rats. I like to imagine Greek spies stealing in and trying to snag a few cats: they are not so easy to catch.

In the Middle Ages cats became associated with witches and were burned, buried alive and otherwise cruelly mistreated. This in turn helped the rat-carrying plagues of that period to decimate populations.

Today cat shows are held all over the land and cat breeding has become big business. Country cats are respected and cherished, and animal shelters pick up the unwanted kittens some summer people toss from their cars as they head back to what they feel is civilization.

But there are still some misunderstandings about cat nature. Many people think all cats are alike. The same people will discuss the difference between a hunting dog and a toy poodle, both of which are dogs. When they buy a dog, they will not get an Irish setter if they live on the top floor of a big city apartment house; they will get what I call an inside dog, one that needs a minimum of exercise.

But when it comes to cats, these same people feel all cats are alike. A cat is a cat. Cats are indifferent and solitary, they say. Cats do not care for anybody. They cannot be taught anything. They cannot be trusted. You must never leave them alone with a baby.

I do not know where the superstition arose that cats will suck a baby's breath and should never be left alone with a baby. This is absolute nonsense. Amber, for instance, tiptoes up to a baby and goes so far as to sniff the nearest minute foot waving in the air (she is a great sniffer). Then she folds herself up and contemplates this fascinating phenomenon.

Most cats seem to realize that a baby is somehow human although in a diminished version. Some feel protective and some retire to the nearest ample lap to watch from a secure distance. Even cats who are afraid of

*Esmé and Tigger. The Siamese is beautiful and uninhibited;
the Manx is sensible as a banker.*

jumping-jack older children apparently understand that the baby-carriage set is not going to grab them suddenly.

As for "indifferent" and "solitary" Amber only smiled when I told her this (both cats and dogs smile). "Indifferent" and "solitary" do not exactly fit her. Whatever I am doing, she is doing with me and wherever I go I have to watch out not to step on that small form. She just happens to be right there and usually wants to be reassured that I still love her as much as I did ten minutes ago. Sometimes I have to stop whatever chore I am doing and sit down and hold her for twenty minutes while she purrs and spreads her toes.

When I have to leave her and put her in the bedroom, she does not speak a word but stands looking at me with desperate wide eyes. How can you desert me? The anguish of a forever-good-by is in that small face.

As for learning, the fourth time I got out the harness —which meant going for a walk—she jumped on the table and began to purr while I struggled with the buckle. And the first time she traveled to Cape Cod from Connecticut in her carrying case, the five-hour trip did not faze her. She began to investigate the new home with great interest the minute the case was opened.

A few days later, I got out the case to take her to the veterinarian. She tiptoed over, inspected it and then got in, folding her tail around her. I decided, as I lugged the case to the car, that I had an intellectual genius inside.

After two trips to the veterinarian she accepted the whole routine with no struggle. I had seen a cat in the same office who needed three people to hold her down, all of whom bore scars of the conflict. But Amber has an acceptance of inevitability that I wish I could always have.

One cat book I read says the Abyssinian is timid, but I know one who is not. When a friend brought in an elderly cat, Amber stiffened her small self. Her fur rose, doubling her size, and she drew back her lips and hissed until her whiskers vibrated. The hiss was loud as a steam engine. Smutsie, the guest, sat quietly looking at her without twitching an eyelid. Amber added a low menacing sound between hisses and started toward him. She was as deadly as four pounds could ever be against twenty or more.

When I hastily gathered her up, I could feel a heartbeat too fast to count. And Smutsie was removed, still ignoring her.

When a group of strangers comes in, she vanishes briefly, but soon that small triangular face pokes around the corner and she looks the gathering over. She makes her choice, which is usually a man, and shortly is perched on his shoulder from which it is easy to reach down when he holds up a sliver of sharp Cheddar cheese. I notice that even if he happens to be indifferent to cats, he begins to talk to her and then, of course, to rub her behind the ears. Her purr joins the conversation.

However, when the voices climb to that unfortunate level so typical of parties, she finds the noise too much for her sensitive ears and retires to the quiet of my bedroom. When the group thins out, she is ready to come back and be admired again.

I have one very dear friend who has a cat phobia. The first time she came over after Amber arrived, I did not know this, so Amber was on the sofa industriously washing herself. This time she did *not* go over to the guest, she minded her own laundry. Later, the friend said if she could ever like a cat, it would be Amber.

The customary picture of a cat is one of serenity. There is usually a fireplace and the cat is folded up in front of it. Or the cat dozes on a wide window sill. Amber's idea is to get as close to the fire as is safe and then to jump up and down as the flames leap. On the window sill she swivels her small head so as to see everything outside, always hoping a bird may fly past so she can start quivering and chittering. There is nothing somnolent about her, whether she is smelling the roses on the table or bounding after a moth.

There are still people who worry about having a black cat cross their path. This must be a special hangover from the witchcraft days. My Tigger was blacker than Waterman's black ink, but he brought nothing but good luck to Stillmeadow for he was a born mouser and cleaned up the ancient cellar in no time. He also diminished the moles that ate the bulbs and tunneled the lawn. One day he made history in the garden as he inspected a mole hole. He sat with his bullet head cocked for a few minutes and then he moved back and pulled up a length of weed (we always had weeds available). Tiptoeing over, he stuck the weed stem in the edge of the hole and then removed himself a short distance and sat. I had seen this from the kitchen window and called the rest of the family. We could not decide what Tigger was up to, but we found out. When the weed moved, he bolted like black lightning and grabbed the mole.

It was fortunate I had witnesses or everyone would

Esmé, like Amber, was a dainty person.

have said my imagination was working as usual. But the most practical member of the family, Jill, admitted Tigger had planted that weed so that when it moved he would know the mole was coming out. Jill said he was miscast in life and should have been in Wall Street.

Occasionally I meet people who say they could never have a cat because a cat kills birds. None of my cats has been able to fly, and the birds that cloud the sky over Stillmeadow simply soar away when the cats come around.

One of the most unfortunate superstitions about cats is that if you feed them well, they will not catch mice or rats. Some owners actually withhold food so that kitty will get the mice. This is not only cruel but senseless. A well-fed cat has more energy for hunting and does not lose his strong instinct to chase small scurrying creatures.

Rats and mice carry more deadly disease than I can name, including bubonic plague. Recently the government has been embroiled in the problem of rats in city ghettos. Rats spread lice, fleas and mange. They bite babies in their cribs and destroy food, which is not too plentiful in ghettos at best.

Rat control could be possible at minimum expense in all cities, I think. Cats could be obtained from any A.S.P.C.A., which has to destroy so many who have been deserted. If every ghetto family had one cat and an allowance of those catfood pellets that are inexpensive and will keep indefinitely, I feel confident that the rat problem would be solved. This is probably too simple a solution for the government—and would be too inexpensive.

Someone once told me about a Southern town that had

a plague of rats some seventy-five years ago. Then a smart man in a neighboring state advertised rattraps to solve the problem. The rattraps were simply cats. The cats cleaned up the town and only cost a dollar each.

Amber enjoys hunting ants in the yard and moths against the windowpane and an occasional spider. The final pounce is like a meteor on a summer night. She has an unfortunate tendency to swallow the victim before I can fish it out of that delicate pink mouth. But all of these unscheduled snacks seem to agree with her, so I tell myself to stop worrying and concentrate instead on her marvelous hunting skill.

Chapter 3

To Amber, daily life is always exciting. On Cape Cod it is especially so. The house on Mill Pond is not so isolated as Stillmeadow, and people drop in at all hours of the day and night. There is a sign at the front door which says PLEASE DO NOT LET THE CAT OUT OF THE DOOR. So visitors peer through the glass timidly and then venture to open a small crack in the door and call nervously, "Is it all right to come in?"

I swoop Amber up until the door is closed again. Only the grocery boy and the milkman are agile enough to get through by themselves without having Amber go with them. Most cats, fortunately, can be let out to run free. Very often my friend Petie decides to go out at midnight on a good moon-bright night. But he can take care of himself. The cat next door, who was not so intelligent, was run over as he was crossing the road in the middle of the afternoon.

Certainly Amber is not equipped to fend for herself in the big outside. A small cat cannot get out of the way of danger and is hard to find if she gets lost. I was especially thankful that Amber was inside last night when I saw a stately enormous skunk walking sedately down the steps. A skunk is no menace if you leave him alone, but Amber's curiosity is boundless. She never leaves anything or anybody alone. And one real encounter with a skunk might even blind her.

There are also stray dogs who would love to chase her to a treetop. The Rescue Squad might not like to bring extension ladders too often to retrieve one small cat. Country cats, like Tigger, can climb high into a tree and sit on a branch for a long time and then descend easily. But house cats like Aladdin and Amber can get up very well but never seem able to figure out how to get down again.

Theoretically, you could train any cat to climb down a tree by backing him down paw by paw, holding on to him firmly. But I have never attempted this, partly because the cat is always too high to reach and partly because he is usually so scared he tightens his hold on that top branch, while he screams.

Walking on a leash is a different matter altogether.

Amber's training began with a collar which a neighbor gave her. I put it on her and went to answer the telephone. By the time I hung up, Amber was also hung up on the collar. She had her lower jaw hooked under the leather and was rapidly strangling. Before I got it off we were both near death's door. I decided immediately that collars are for dogs but not for cats. At least my cats.

Subsequently I heard of other cats whose collars caught on branches or hooks or whose paws had been damaged by being caught in the collar as the cats tried to claw it off.

29

The idea of belling a cat does not appeal to me because this would make any cat nervous as well as warning mice or stray dogs as to just where the cat is.

I never had a dog who was bothered by a collar. The argument against harnesses has always been that they tend to spread the shoulders, and show dogs never wear them. When I thought it over, I doubted whether Amber would really have her shoulders spread by a small light harness if I didn't haul her around by it.

I began by leaving the harness on the floor so she could investigate the buckles and clasp. Then I put it on her and left it for five minutes, letting her run around the floor and pull the leash. I followed this procedure for several days and then I carried her out of doors with the harness on and set her on the grass. I kept the leash loose. The first time she just stood on tiptoe with quivering whiskers. The second time she took a few steps. The third time she caught an ant. The fourth time I said, "Want to go outdoors?" and she jumped to the corner of the table by the door and waited, purring loudly, for the harness to be put on.

Now all I have to do is ask the question and she flies onto the table and pokes her nose at the harness. So she has learned one whole sentence—"Want to go outdoors?" In fact, if I am telling someone that I plan to take Amber for a walk soon, I have to spell the words. And even when I spell them she somehow happens to be on the harvest table, just in case.

In general, I do not think words as words will ever mean as much to her as to the dogs, but she knows enough for her purposes. "I am going to fix you something to eat" is an easy one. "I have to go down to the

Tigger was a great mouser.
Amber met only one rat and demolished him.

village for the mail but I'll be back soon," is understandable.

The tone of voice is more important to her than words, however. She reacts with pleasure to compliments no matter what the words are because of the heart-warming tone. I experimented by telling her she was just impossible but in an admiring tone, and she purred and kneaded her paws and was delighted.

Harsh sounds bother her. The rotary mower going at a neighbor's makes her nervous, as it does me. The sound of a jet plane flattens her ears. But thunder is only mildly bothersome to Amber, whereas it terrified several of my dogs.

Any sudden crash sends her high in the air. I dropped a broiler pan the other day in the kitchen and Amber really levitated. But she came out immediately afterward to see what was going on. The sound of a small child screeching drives her under the nearest bed, but she pokes a wary nose out before long to see what it is all about.

Cats hear sounds even beyond the range of a dog's ears, and a dog is said to have a range of twenty-five thousand cycles a second. The human has fifteen thousand. With this extrasensitivity, any harsh sound must be painful.

Amber has no difficulty in distinguishing the sounds of various automobile motors. She knows our friend Margaret Stanger's car very well, and when it draws up, she flies to the door ready for the treat that always comes with Margaret. The grocery truck sends her to the kitchen, in case there may be a steak in the carton. When a strange car drives up, she tenses and stands ready to seek refuge in the bedroom until she knows who has come. But the retreat is brief and she emerges on tentative paws to inspect the intruders.

Purses are fun to explore and she tries to push the clasps with her nose. There might be morsels of chicken or beef inside for a cat who is starved by a cruel owner. If a jacket has any kind of fringe, like Scotch plaid, she chews the fringe and usually gets a strand or two of wool before she is discovered.

I understand that some biologists are experimenting with communication between animals and man by spoken words. I may say I doubt the value of most of the experiments conducted on domestic animals because no laboratory can reproduce the natural conditions of living as a part of the family. When I say "careful" to Amber as she is biting my hand in an excess of affection, she does chew more gently, but I candidly cannot say I think the word "careful" is the reason. I think it is the warning, admonitory tone of my voice she responds to.

It was on Mill Pond when I first discovered how far Amber can see. I am farsighted myself, but long after I cannot glimpse the flight of a gull, Amber follows it with nose lifted, eyes shining, tail lashing. She swivels her head to catch the last wing-beat out to the sea. Often she will inform me a bird is coming inland, and eventually I see it myself.

In bright daylight, her eyes are topaz with a dark slit of pupil (which cuts down the intensity of the light). As afternoon draws on, the pupil grows larger and more oval-shaped and by dusk her eyes are onyx. If all the clocks stopped I could almost tell the time of day by her eyes. At night, her eyes shine, and I am told this is because there is an iridescent layer of cells there which we do not have and which reflect light we cannot see.

This again suggests inheritance, for cats in the beginning were probably nocturnal, and I know quite a few who still are, really wanting to begin to live just as the tired owner is ready to drop from fatigue. Fortunately for me, Amber does not prowl all night. Perhaps if I retired at a reasonable hour it would be different, but I usually stay up quite late. She stays up too and we both watch television.

Her favorite hour is the weather report. As the weatherman assumes his academic pose before a generally troubled-looking map, she folds herself into a compact ball on the back of the armchair. And then he raises the pointer—oh lovely moment—and she springs into the air and soars across the room. On tiptoe, she tries to catch the tip of the pointer. As the weatherman, smiling, predicts hurricanes or floods, Amber is all over the map with him. She works so hard that when the report is over, she has to wash herself.

She also enjoys some musical hours, especially those with horns such as the Tijuana Brass. With a Bernstein concert, she may doze through part of a symphony, but when the camera pans to the violin section she is wide awake.

My television habits have changed slightly since Amber came to stay. I never used to watch wild-animal shows or circus acts with little dogs dressed in petticoats and walking on their hind legs. Now I have to turn on jungle-adventure programs for her, as well as the variety shows that have performing animals.

Perhaps the most exciting show she has seen was one which showed a lioness with her cubs. Amber knocked an ash tray from the table while leaning over the edge to watch one cub leap around.

The reason I find this surprising is that the cockers and Irish never bothered much with television, and I assumed they felt the world would be as well off without that silly screen. But Amber even finds radio interesting and often pokes around behind the small set trying to discover where the sound is born.

When the TV set is finally turned off at night, Amber has a wild race, tearing through the house, leaping from chair top to window sills and back again. Then she is ready to go to sleep and curls up until she is no larger than a baby's mitten. Her seal-dark tail folds around her and her apricot nose rests under tucked paws. I wish human beings could fall instantly to sleep the way cats can. The moment she is folded up comfortably she is sound asleep.

If I get up in the night to check a banging window or tighten a faucet, she opens one eye and yawns. She implies that I am silly to wake up after we are all settled down for the night.

If Amber gets up before I do in the morning, she is so quiet I do not know it. I doubt whether any animal can be as noiseless as a kitten. I have to see Amber to believe in her. About nine thirty she decides it is time to start the day, and she jumps on my pillow with helicopter purrs and spreading paws. She even sometimes gives me an encouraging lick, and if that fails, a soft bite.

Her tongue feels like warm fine sandpaper and is

surprisingly strong. The top is textured, with tiny hooks, which is why Amber can keep her fur so clean, for the hooks literally comb out the fur.

When I look at her with her face so close, I can see her golden eyelashes. They are invisible to a casual glance, partly because her silvery whiskers are so noticeable. These have very sharp nerves at the roots and are better than man-made antennas for receiving messages. Anyone who trims a cat's whiskers should spend some time in a jail cell.

If I stroke Amber's whiskers, moving my hand gently back from her muzzle, they feel as delicate as cobweb lace. But when she investigates something strange, they quiver vibrantly. I always think I should like to count them, but I get distracted trying to time her purrs!

Amber's purrs are a mystery. They vary in intensity from a drowsy thread of sound to a deep full throb when I get out her harness. Sometimes they are rapid and sometimes light as dew. The experts seem to agree on only one thing, which is that the cat is the only animal which purrs. But they do not know why.

Purring begins at the age of a week. Does the mother teach the kittens? Or does something just develop in the vocal cords or elsewhere in the throat? And what relation does this have to prehistoric times when the first cats roamed the jungles?

The earliest purr is a monotone, but later on two purr tones may be heard, even three. The sound is happiness distilled. A purring kitten can comfort the sad heart like music.

On the other hand, a miaow is one of the saddest sounds I have ever heard. But the miaow itself is varied.

Country kittens can take care of themselves.

The hunger miaow is thin and sharp. The miaow when danger seems imminent is louder and wilder. Then Amber also has a questioning miaow which means she is bored and wants me to do something about it. Fortunately I have rarely heard the miaow of pain which has a desperate screeching tone.

There is one time Amber never uses her voice. When a stranger comes to the door she is absolutely silent. If she decides this is not a friend, she stiffens her slight self and raises every hair until her tail balloons and there is a ridge down her back. Her whiskers quiver and she stands on tiptoe. Most dogs utter at least a tentative bark when someone comes to the door, and mine always wagged their tails at the same time. But Amber lets me know someone is coming simply by standing and swelling!

The language of Amber's tail is eloquent. When she is happy, her tail stands straight up like a slim flagpole. When she waves it back and forth slowly, it means she will have more brushing, please. If she is asked to take a pill, the tail whips violently. And when a bird or rabbit comes too near the window, it lashes even more forcibly.

Communication is never static. People who love one another communicate by an expression, a lift of the eyebrow, a touch of the hand. Words are scarcely necessary. This is also true when you live with an animal you love. Every day Amber and I understand each other better and communicate with more ease. But developing this understanding rests with the owner. If you consider your cat just a convenient mousetrap, you will never have any other relationship.

Chapter 4

Living with a kitten or cat is a rewarding experience. Like dogs, they ask so little and give so much. And they still carry within themselves so many traits that have come down from the ancient past.

Man has had for thousands of years what the biologists call a symbiotic relationship with certain other species, which means that both live together for their mutual benefit. It is not exactly fair because we are always at the top and the animal has to adjust to us. We have seldom, if ever, tried to maintain this symbiosis on a fair basis.

We began the association for our own uses. Dogs could chase the primitive hunter's prey and bring it in and receive a bone for reward. Cats could keep down the rat and mouse population, not to mention moles and other small predators, and in return get a few inches by the fire to curl up in.

We had the best of both worlds, using the skill of our symbiotic associates but feeling no responsibility in return. Now we are supposed to be highly civilized creatures, although we alone deliberately kill our own kind, the lower animals do not—except perhaps in the heat of sexual competition.

In the long history of mankind, dogs have been easiest to subjugate. A dog will put up with almost anything. Dogs have infinite patience with this peculiar breed that controls their destinies and will even wear skirts and headdresses and run around on their hind legs to amuse people.

Cats, on the other hand, have managed to keep a kind of independence. They are determined to preserve a little of their original personality. This is the reason so many people say they would never have a cat because a cat is unmanageable. As one who loves and admires both dogs and cats, I may say this is exceedingly silly. We do not expect everyone to be exactly alike, and if we feel a cat should be like a dog, we are missing something important.

For instance, I never had a dog who felt it was vital to leap to the mantelpiece or swing on the Venetian-blind cords. But I am always picking Amber out of the milk-glass cupboard or disentangling her claws from the fringe of the bedspread.

I also fish her out of my desk drawer before I forget and close it. I watch the refrigerator to be sure she hasn't slipped in when the door swung open. I expect her to spend more time in the air than on the floor because she is, by inheritance, a climbing and leaping creature. As far as she is concerned, the floor is a take-off place for the upper regions.

I notice she has a definite route for anywhere in the house, and I marvel that her small head holds so many exact maps. And she seldom has to set a paw on the floor. In the beginning, she fell once, trying to leap from one kitchen counter to another across the room. She was ashamed and showed it. She thought it over and the next time made an interim landing on a chair back. I now have to be sure that this one high-backed chair is never out of place. People who expect their pets to stay right on the floor should never live with a cat.

In prehistoric days the cat family must have lived a great deal in trees, which were both a refuge and a vantage point for attack. Dogs never climbed trees so far as we know. So if you find you are nervous when four delicate paws land in the middle of the worktable, you do not need a cat.

I find Amber's aerial quality a delight! Perhaps I wouldn't feel as I do if I were an Olympic pole vaulter or skier, but as I make my pedestrian way about the house I love to watch Amber leaping from window sill to sofa back, from chair back to the top of the cupboard that reaches almost to the ceiling. The incredible grace of movement and the freedom satisfy a deep need in me. It gives me a sense of weightlessness which perhaps the astronauts enjoy.

I also love the extra companionship which results. I like to start typing and have a beautiful apricot kitten make a perfect landing in the middle of my desk or to be scrubbing the sink and suddenly find an interested wedge-shaped face beside me as Amber balances on the narrow edge of the sink. If I sit by the fire to read, a small person lands soundlessly on the chairback and someone is purring in my ear.

Then we come to the controversial problem of birds.

In the days of the cave dwellers cats ate birds, it is said, and I see no reason to deny this. It may not fit in with my devotion to birds to realize that the three wild, country cats in my yard are there mainly because the bird feeder is there. They wait for their natural heritage.

Amber certainly never has to worry about where her next meal is coming from. It is coming from the refrigerator and will be warmed on the stove. However, as she sits on the kitchen window sill and watches the sparrows on the well house, a curious thing happens. She begins to make an odd chittering sound. The pulse in her throat beats rapidly. Her lips draw back and quiver and her whiskers tremble. Her tail switches. Her body is tense. Her sharp teeth are visible, which they almost never are.

She is merely repeating the pattern set thousands of years ago, and she feels deep within her that those twittering birds are prey. I doubt whether she could ever catch a bird, for she has had no training in the art. But the feeling is there. And I respect it.

We all have basic instincts which we have inherited from the beginning of our breed. Since we have no fur covering as the rest of the mammals have, we must have warmth. When we sit around the applewood fire at Stillmeadow, we are happy because it gives us a feeling of protection, and if the furnace heat is too much we open a few doors to cool the house so we can still toast ourselves by the leaping flames. I have seen tense and troubled people sink down on the couch and look at the hearth and sigh with relief.

We must have food, and although now we buy it at supermarkets, the hunting instinct is still with us. If we

Amber never goes out alone.

gather the sweet, dark wild strawberries or high bush blueberries or hunt for Morel mushrooms, we revert to the prehistoric times when men fed on wild fruits and berries. The hunter who boasts of getting his deer has satisfied the same instinct. As for the fisherman who sits all day in a boat, broiling in the sun or soaked with rain, just to bring in a few fish, he too is a happy throwback. He may spend countless sums on fishing tackle and the boat, but in his bones he feels he is providing fish for the family.

We also have an instinct to provide shelter for the young. It may be a small cabin or a mansion, but as soon as people have children, they wish to give up any nomadic existence they once enjoyed and maintain a homeplace. I have noticed that though the Hollywood stars, the theatre people, the musicians depend mainly on hotel living and jet travel, they always speak with pride of their homes. Sometimes they have several in different places, obviously so they will have a home wherever they go.

Most of us have basic fears too. Snakes and spiders seem high on the list. It is not really rational to be afraid of either except in tropical places. But the smallest green snake in the yard at Stillmeadow can throw a guest into fits. I myself do not like spiders and feel sure some ancestor was bitten by a large hairy poisonous spider.

When you consider how much we react as our early forebears did, we should not blame our house pets if they respond to their own heritage. It is not a sin for a cat to chase a bird. And it is wrong to punish a cat who manages to get a bird. The reason my cats never have is because the birds are so healthy around here and have plenty of sense. My cats have settled for moles and mice. Actually a bird has a marvelous awareness of danger and can be airborne too fast for a cat to catch it.

However, I do not plan to let Amber try her skill with the birds I feed. And I doubt whether she would be very energetic in pursuit since she dines so well right on the kitchen counter. A homeless hungry cat may be able to snare a bird who cannot take off fast enough, and thus survive for another day or two.

Flies are Amber's chief prey. She will try to climb the wall when a fly buzzes around. So I assume that in the early days, cats also ate small flying insects as well as birds.

But in case she ever does catch a bird, I shall not greet her with cries that she is a bad, bad girl and shame on her. I shall realize that she is a product of evolution as I am but that we haven't evolved in quite the same direction. (Wouldn't most of our mammals look on a human battle line with absolute disbelief!)

When I began to write about Amber, I made the statement that she would probably never see a mouse and would have no idea what it was. But one evening when I had been working late I went to the kitchen for a snack, and there in the middle of the doorway was a half-grown rat, composed in death. He was nearly as big as Amber. She was prancing around with her tail like a wind-blown flag and was obviously stuffed with pride.

Somehow the rat had found a way to get in the cellar and had come up a drain pipe and into the ancient corner cupboard which houses the milk glass.

Amber flew over to show me where she had found him.

The remarkable thing was that there was not a scar of battle on her small fragile person and there had been no sound. If I had known about it, I might have had a heart attack and would certainly have made a mess of things trying to rescue my darling and prevent her from protecting our house.

As it was, I praised her extravagantly, wrapped the rat in a paper towel and laid him in the woodshed to show Connie and Curt when they came for the weekend. I did not want them to think Mamma was imagining things!

The amazing thing was that Amber knew exactly how to attack and kill this monster although she had never had any experience except with a catnip toy mouse. Somehow she reached instantly into her heritage and instinctively found the skill, not to mention the strength, to dispatch her hereditary foe.

However, she had no idea of dragging her victim to a secret lair. She wanted me to admire her victory and present her with a special dish of diced chicken.

(Photography by Gordon S. Smith)

Amber might have been named Topaz. . . .

Chapter 5

Recently I read that there are ten million cats in the United States, which means five million more cats than dogs. I always wonder how experts arrive at these round figures. Even as they estimate, more puppies are turning blind noses to the daylight and thimble-sized kittens are reaching for the first mouthful of warm life-giving milk. So who knows?

But the preponderance of cats does suggest that the cat can take care of himself better than a dog. A cat can pry open a garbage can and fish out something or sneak in an alleyway and find a mouse or rat. A homeless dog either starves or gets run over or shot by some ambitious hunter. In the city, a cat can jump from one apartment-house roof to another. A dog cannot even get up there. Also, a chased cat can vanish as no dog can. In my part of the country, an unlicensed dog is picked up and, if no home is found, is destroyed. But nobody pays any attention to the cats that live off the land and do not wear licenses.

The country cats that visit my yard would never

submit to a collar and license. Sometimes I wonder what would happen if cats had to have licenses—spayed female so much, altered male so much, unspayed females more, etc. I would very much like to have Amber registered at the Town Hall and listed with a number and my address, but I realize wearing a small metal tag would drive her crazy.

It would also, again, involve a collar to hang the license on. A harness would be useless because when the harness is used, the owner is there. Recently I met a charming Golden Retriever puppy shipped from Canada and he had a serial number for identification tattooed on one ear.

But a Golden has firm thick ears, whereas no cat has ears thick enough to tattoo. And the Golden could not tell me whether this hurt a good deal at the time or not. It is, however, a permanent insurance against anyone stealing a valuable dog, whereas dog stealers toss collars away as they go about their business of marketing stolen dogs.

So far, I cannot think of any way to attach a label and phone number to a cat!

Advertisements for lost dogs usually give the license number, but advertisements for lost cats are pathetic. "Lost in the vicinity of————one spayed female with white paws and a white forefront. Answers to the name of Baby." Since Baby is not apt to rush up to a stranger, this is not very helpful.

Also cats do not identify so readily with a name. Amber comes when I call her either Amber or Sweetheart. But since she is nearly always underfoot, calling her is seldom necessary except when she gets shut in a closet. Then I wish that when I call *"Amber"* she would call back instead of just sitting in the dark and waiting.

Esmé knew her name very well but paid no attention unless she was on her way already. And Tigger, the Manx, would turn his green-glass eyes to me and imply I was very silly because I could see him, couldn't I?

This curious indifference to a label may be peculiar to Amber. She understands very well when I say "Let's go for a walk." Or, "I have something for you to eat —come in the kitchen." Or, "I am going for the mail but I shall be right back." And, as I have said, she knows what the word No means. After one nibble of the best African violet, she waits for that No.

I talk to her about everything and would advise any cat owner to do the same with his cat. Too many cat owners accept a cat's apparent indifference to special commands. Since I have lived with Amber, I know the variations in her voice and can understand almost everything she tries to tell me. I think this is reciprocal. Otherwise when I explain I am going to the typewriter to work, why does she fly ahead of me and jump on the machine and begin pushing the buttons to see the keys hop up?

And even when I don't talk to her, Amber understands what I am thinking. When I have to shut her in the bedroom preparatory to my going out, I have to sneak in and turn the rug back so the door will close. I try not to have her observe this tactic. If she sees me shove the rug over, she vanishes and I am late for the party because I can't find her.

"Well, this is a surprise," one friend said as I turned up ten minutes late for dinner, "you are always so early

Stairs are for climbing.

(Jacques Chepard)

we just rush to get ready and even so we are always late. But here *you* are! Late."

"Amber didn't want to be left alone," I explained.

When I get back I call from the front door, "I'm back, Sweetheart!"

She is at the door of the bedroom, yawning. She has been asleep on the pillow and probably hasn't missed me at all, but she is like an actor in the third act of a play. She rises to the drama of my coming home and not abandoning her forever. Jumping around, purring, kneading her paws, rubbing her head against my hand, twitching her tail and putting an occasional melancholy miaow in the middle of a purr. She has, she implies, suffered excruciatingly.

Which brings me to the point of sleeping. A puppy who is left alone may yell his head off until his lips are foam-flecked. He may claw the door, tear up the furniture and make a career of suffering. When he is older, he gets over this. A kitten goes to sleep. This is partly because cats sleep more than dogs. Recently I read another one of those doubtful statements to the effect that a cat may sleep seventeen hours a day.

If so, it is because a cat exercises violently and completely. The acrobatics of a kitten remind me of Ringling's circus. After Amber goes at a dizzying speed, up in the air, the whole length of the house, for half an hour, she takes a nap with paws folded under her chin, tail quiescent.

A hunting dog may run all day and after a brief rest be ready for an automobile ride. But he does not use every muscle in his body the way a cat does. He seldom leaps, climbs, swings in the air; he just runs through brush. This observation is purely my own without benefit of experts.

The agility of a kitten is amazing until you get used to it. I watch Amber and decide this is the nearest thing to flying without wings. Also, she uses a lot of energy washing, which involves one hind leg at an acute angle while she scrubs, the head swiveled completely while she works at her ears. Her muscles seem to be fluent. The one place she cannot reach is behind her head between the ears, so I give special attention to that and she thanks me with a large enthusiastic purr.

When Amber is asleep, she is motionless as a figurine. This interests me because the dogs always dreamed. Holly, the Irish, would twitch her paws as if she were running a race and often wag her plumed tail wildly. She was a happy dreamer. Amber is quiet as still water. I have been told that all mammals dream (and perhaps birds too) and that the mind is eased by working things out while we sleep. If this is so, I conclude that Amber keeps her dreams inside her mind without reacting physically. The absolute repose of a sleeping cat somehow eases the tensions of a watcher. Often I reach out and touch Amber to be sure she is still warmly alive.

Amber wakes instantly. She may yawn once widely and then she is leaping-active. My cockers and Irish yawned and stretched and yawned again with sleepy-lidded eyes. I belong to this type myself, for the first hour I am up is like being on a slow boat to China, as it were.

But one interesting thing about Amber's sleep is that the slightest sound alerts her. Occasionally I can tiptoe past a dog-tired dog, but if I get up noiselessly in the night for a drink of water, Amber is already on the bathroom bowl, leaning over the faucet to catch the first drip when I turn it on. And when I move silently to the wing at the Cape to work at the typewriter, I often think she is sound asleep on the bed. But when I get to the wing, she is already perched on the carriage of my machine.

Finally, as to sleep, cats like secret places some of the time. Dogs usually choose their own bed and never sleep anywhere else. But Amber may emerge from the linen closet or the kitchen cupboard. She has two kitten houses, one especially made by the grandchildren and one bought at a fancy pet store and equipped with a rug and an upper porch, but she almost never uses them. I have learned when I open a drawer never to close it entirely in case she has slipped in for a nap. Or I may find her tucked in the bookshelves, warmed by Keats and Shakespeare.

Once I closed the closet door in the wing and went peacefully to bed, assuming she was in the chair by the open fire. In the morning I called her and had no answer and began a frantic search. After combing the whole house, I opened that one closet door and out came Amber, a little cross at being confined in there all night but otherwise quite self-possessed. Now I leave that door ajar too, for her melancholy confinement did *not* give her a horror of the closet. It is full of fine things to play with, she says.

The one place where she never lies down is the right half of the best sofa. Even if I am sitting on that sofa at the other end, she leaps from the table to my side without invading the right end, which was Holly's. Since she never saw Holly, there can be no memory pattern, and certainly none of that sweet-hay scent of an Irish is left, so I am happy to assume that Amber has an understanding with Holly herself.

In our Connecticut house a lot has happened. The previous owner murdered his wife one night and then committed suicide, which must have been hard on their houseguest, who had come to the country to visit them after a nervous breakdown. My own feeling about the household ghosts is that they are companionable. They all, in their time, loved Stillmeadow. No matter what tragedies they endured, the fact that this house was cherished is evident in every hand-hewn stone and hand-cut beam. But I wondered about Amber who is so very sensitive.

At first when she heard footsteps and nobody was there, her ears went out like wind-blown sails. A ridge of fur rose along her backbone. Occasionally she uttered a faint hiss. But before long she was only curious and interested. Sometimes around two in the morning she stands on tiptoe at the foot of the old pineapple-post bed. She rests her triangle of chin on the footboard and stares wide-eyed through the bedroom door into the family room beyond. When the footsteps cease, she yawns and tucks up again on my pillow.

The only time she objected was one night when suddenly two books flung themselves from the top shelf in the bedroom. They were books dating back to 1800, bound in ancient leather. One was *Poems of Old Age* and one *Poems for a Young Man*. I have no idea whose they were in the beginning, but they landed on the maple daybed with muffled bangs, and Amber leaped six inches in the air.

Most of the animals that have owned me have had perceptions I could not have. When they prowl around nervously, I stop whatever I am doing and look to see what has gone wrong in the house. When they jump on the window sill and look earnestly down the road, I take off my apron and powder my face hastily. Long before the sound of a motor is heard, they *know*. But if the car coming down the road is not going to stop at Stillmeadow or Still Cove, as the case may be, they pay no attention.

Amber, naturally, does not bark but she is a good watcher. She jumps up and down, tail flashing back and forth. She unfurls her ears and points in the direction of the menace. If she hears the car of her favorite friend Margaret Stanger, she flies to the door, purring up a storm. Margaret always brings a snack. One time, though, she came directly from a party where she couldn't sneak even a morsel in her purse. Amber tried to open the purse, then went through the pockets of Margaret's sweater, and then sat down and miaowed pitifully. A week or so later, Margaret telephoned to say that she had started over to my house and got as far as the nearest neighbor's, but then realized she had forgotten Amber's snack so she turned around and went home.

This probably proves that a small kitten has no difficulty managing her subjects!

But I must add that the subjects are more flattered when she flies into their laps and spreads her paws and

Amber always prefers Christmas-tree decorations to toys.

rubs her head against them and purrs and purrs than they would be if Queen Elizabeth awarded them something to hang around their necks.

Amber's self-appointed role as watchcat always surprises me. With Esmé, the Siamese, her reaction to strangers at the door was to spin upstairs and hide in the bathroom. Tigger, the Manx, sat by the fire and scrubbed his blunt square face no matter who came in. But Amber hears a car coming far down the road. She always recognizes the sound of friends' cars, as I have said, although she had some trouble when Margaret bought a new one. The first time Margaret came in from that car Amber jumped on the harvest table and stared with disbelief. It took several minutes before she hurried over to say hello. The second or third time the car pulled in the drive, Amber was at the kitchen window waiting.

When a strange car turns down our road, Amber rushes to the front door and lashes her tail. If she thinks I have not noticed it—and I often haven't—she dashes in and jumps on my desk and then runs back to her watch-point.

Naturally she could never fall on an intruder and mangle him as a dog could. She cannot bark a warning. Even when she hisses you have to listen hard to hear her. But I feel perfectly secure with Amber to notify me someone is coming and which door he or she is coming toward and whether he or she is familiar or not. Furnace men, painters, electricians she greets with joy. But one night a strange man came to the door. He was trying to deliver a package from the next town and was hopelessly lost. Amber greeted his arrival like a miniature leopard (all five pounds of her).

No German Shepherd could be a more dedicated guardian of the home than this small Abyssinian kitten.

Chapter 6

Amber was three and a half months old when she came to Stillmeadow. When I picked her up, it was like holding a handful of milkweed fluff. I felt she must have been the size of a golden thimble when she was born. A kitten, according to the books, should be at least seven weeks old before leaving the mother. By then the kitten has been trained by the mother in sanitary habits and can go on a basic diet served in a crystal bowl.

The proper diet for a cat seems to be a controversial subject. I had a list from the breeder which I approved of and I also read my whole shelf of cat books. Hardly one agreed with another, which shows that cat people have much in common with dog people! I agreed with Dr. Leon Whitney who believes cats should have vegetables in the diet. While some people feel cats must be meat—or fish—eaters exclusively, Leon points out that cats who live on rats or mice get predigested vegetables in the innards of the prey. He also points out that cats have been domesticated for thousands of years more than many mammals and are adapted to life in man's world.

I started Amber on baby food—lamb and vegetables, beef and vegetables, liver and vegetables, chicken and broth. I omitted those gay jars of bacon and vegetables since ham and bacon, and probably any variety of pork, do not seem to me advisable for a kitten. I also gave her warm milk on the side. Since liver and milk are presumably laxative, I kept them at a minimum since she arrived troubled with diarrhea, possibly because she had roundworms.

I must digress and say that any puppy or kitten should be checked for worms. Even in the days when we raised litters of cocker puppies in the most sanitary conditions, now and then roundworms would turn up. When they are four weeks old, it is time to check. Worming nowadays is very simple with modern drugs, and Amber never lost a meal.

I think a varied diet is better for cats, just as I believe in it for dogs. Man himself in the prehistoric days presumably ate raw meat when he was lucky, but man became omnivorous as the centuries rolled on, and the two who have lived closest to him, dogs and cats, have adapted to changing circumstances in their physical requirements. I have never known a cocker or an Irish who would have survived if he had to kill game and subsist on what he caught. Even country cats that are on their own find supplements in milk in the cowbarns, leftovers around garbage cans, scraps tossed from cars. They nibble sweet fresh grass. If they wander to the town dump, they add a good many odd things to their diet. We keep a pan of kibbled food by the well house for visitors.

There are two digestive differences, however, between cats and humans. I found out at once that Amber's front teeth are sabre-sharp and designed for tearing. Cats normally tear their food and gulp it. Human beings, if they are not starving, chew their food with those flat back teeth. This means starchy food or nuts are pulverized and digest easily. Amber gulps, dipping her head down, throwing her head back and swallowing with a rippling movement in her throat. She even gulped the first baby food, which is already puréed.

The second difference in the cat's digestive system is that the cat does not have the efficient starch-digesting enzyme which human beings have. So starchy meals are not advisable unless the starch is precooked and easily digested.

But I soon discovered that Amber has her own ideas about the need for some starch. I left part of a stuffed baked potato on the table when I went to answer the phone one night, and when I came back, Amber was innocently scrubbing her face and only the potato skin was left. Now when I have baked potato, I put a teaspoonful of it in her dish.

We live in a vitamin-loving age, but a good basic and varied diet provides, in my opinion, enough vitamins. However, a small amount of something like viosterol or a similar type of vitamin mixture may be advisable, and the veterinarian will suggest his preference. When you adopt a starving kitten, vitamin therapy is needed, but it is better to have the veterinarian prescribe than to go to the drugstore and pick out something yourself.

At one time when Amber was still recovering from worms, I made an extra trip to Kim Schneider, the Cape Cod veterinarian adored by patients and owners. He pulled a small tube from his magic cabinet and suggested that Amber should have some extra vitamins until she was fully on her paws again.

When I took the cap from the tube, Amber advanced with interest; and as I squeezed some of the dark substance out to dab on her paws, she put out her minute pink tongue and licked the tube. This, she said, was delicious! So after that I simply called her, took the cap off and squeezed one-sixth of an inch out, and she polished both tube-end and cap.

Now all I do is pick up the tube and call, "Amber, time for vitamins!"

Even when she is busiest she comes flying, and I have to be careful not to squeeze out too much. She would eat a quarter of the tube if she had the chance.

Nobody as far as I know has ever done a study of the modern advances in pet medication, but I am an ardent admirer of the men who have worked in this area. Having spent a good deal of time trying to persuade cockers and Irish that milk of magnesia and such remedies really were fit to swallow, then mopping myself and the floor, I am grateful for a tube of laxative from which a suspicious kitten will take a nice swallow.

When we had thirty-five cockers and two Irish and two cats, I had a whole medicine cabinet stocked for them, and not one single type of medicine was really appealing! Fortunately dogs are easier to persuade than cats, and it is not hard to pull out that lower lip and tuck the medicine in. Amber's lower lip would never pull out. And her throat is so small that only Doctor Kim could ever treat her without a strangle.

The diet chart that came with Amber is a sensible one. For a kitten, it suggests ground chuck, chicken, very little fish, and not more than once a week. Liver and kidney not more than twice a week plus .03 ounce liquid vitamin daily.

This brings me to the question of fish. My dear friends Millie and Ed have a beautiful domestic short-hair (whose coat looks like that of a Persian), one of the healthiest and loveliest cats I have known. Peter decided at an early age that he only wanted to eat tuna fish. He went further. He only wanted one particular brand of tuna fish. He would condescend, tail waving, to nibble one brand of catfood based on the type of tuna he liked. He would not drink milk, or eat chicken, turkey, steak tidbits. When I am at the Cape, I have dinner every Monday night with Millie and Ed, and for several years we spent hours discussing ways of persuading Petie to eat a more balanced diet. Nothing worked. My experience has been that you can persuade a dog into almost anything if only to please you and keep you from bursting into tears.

But a cat will only eat what he or she feels is desirable. No smacking of lips and cooing will make any difference. With a sick puppy, I have gone so far as to get down on the floor and pretend to eat a spoonful of the food he needed. With a cat, it would be useless. Amber, for instance, would watch me with interest and bat at the spoon but never open her mouth. I know this, and it saved me a lot of energy when I discovered she didn't care for eggs. She does not like them raw with milk or soft-boiled or poached or scrambled. So I hard-cooked one and mixed a quarter teaspoon of it with chicken. This she would tolerate, but without undue enthusiasm.

As far as Petie's diet is concerned, I must point out that he is a wonderful mouser, going far afield for mice since the house does not provide them. All the time we worried about him, he was dining on the vital parts of some mice, including the partly digested material in the intestines, which includes some vegetable material.

Then came the worst winter on record. Suddenly Millie imparted the wonderful news that Petie was eating a can of kidney or beef at one sitting plus half a dozen snacks a day. It seems to me reasonable to suppose that with a sudden shortage of the food he got for himself, he sensibly decided that he would eat some of the junk his devoted mistress and master kept urging on him.

However, in view of Petie's addiction to one brand of tuna, I felt I would not start Amber on fish. When she was used to a variety of other things would be time enough. She would never be a mouser, I thought, or an outdoor-country cat. But I discovered how she felt about fish when I dished up a plate of creamed Alaskan King Crab and she tried to get in the plate. I settled for a teaspoon and a promise that life would hold more fish later on. Especially, I said, after she ate her lamb and spinach.

Cats do need some fat. Farm cats manage to get about 25 per cent of fat in their diet. House cats get some in the natural course of events. A balanced diet, says Dr. Whitney, allows around 20 per cent fat. Cow's milk has a considerable amount if it is whole milk. Amber enjoys milk, but is not above licking a stick of butter left on the counter if her meals haven't enough fat in them.

Water is essential. Tigger seldom drank any, but he probably dipped his blunt nose in the pond when he was thirsty. House cats should have *fresh* water available, and Amber drinks frequently. Aladdin used to sit under a leaky faucet and catch the drops as they fell and swallow them. Esmé, the Siamese, drank sparingly, but enjoyed beaten egg yolk which provided some liquid.

For a kitten, I was advised to serve the food slightly warm, never directly from the icebox. At first I had a problem with this for one jar of baby food added up to almost three meals for Amber. I did not want to keep heating up the same food. The right amount set in a pan over a low heat instantly dried into a leathery blob, and most of it had to be scraped from the pan. Adding half a spoonful of liquid turned it into soup. After great thought, I solved this by putting the food on a piece of plastic kitchen wrap, folding the edges tight and dropping it into hot water for a couple of minutes.

With regard to the use of regular catfood, I consulted Dr. Whitney. There are dozens of canned catfoods, catfoods in boxes, all sorts of combinations. Some are made of what they call by-products. Some have a good deal of filler. Some are meals-in-one, some are not.

Considering Amber's tendency to diarrhea, Dr. Whitney suggested adding one of two brands of the tiny

Amber's wedge-shaped face is never far away.

pellets. I'll call them Brand A and Brand B. He said if I put them in her dish, she would play with them (B is made in fancy stars and other shapes). Then she would crunch one and finally eat a few.

Amber admitted she enjoyed tossing them around, dropping them on the floor, chasing them all over the kitchen. But crunch she would not. I added the brand of canned catfood Dr. Whitney recommended, and she sat down and stared at me. I put some of the baby strained beef in with it. She licked up the beef, leaving no pellet so much as cracked.

There may be hardy souls who can defeat a small kitten, but I am not one of them. This was what is called an unequal contest, like having the Green Bay Packers play a high-school football team. I opened a can of lobster bisque and put it on to heat for my own lunch after the morning's struggle, and when I dished it up, Amber advanced, purring loudly. I dribbled a spoonful of the bisque over those controversial pellets and then heard the sweetest music in the world, the sound of a definite *crunch*.

So we reached a compromise. The pellets will be mixed with something added that Amber thinks is fit to eat. Chicken, beef, lamb—and of course, lobster bisque —are her favorites. And there is no problem with diarrhea.

In short, every animal is an individual, and feeding cannot be regimented. Just why Holly, the Irish, wanted her food soupy, while Honey, the cocker, insisted on its being chewy and rather dry, I do not know.

When Amber yawns, I realize how tiny her mouth is and what a small aperture provides a throat. She likes her food to be fairly mushy but varied with bits of meat or chicken that she can tear to pieces, holding one end in her paw. This terrified me at first, for I felt sure she would strangle on anything larger than a pinhead.

I do not give Amber bones. I know the veterinarians say that there is a digestive juice in a cat's stomach which is more powerful than that in a human's and that a bone will be softened in around an hour. But a sharp shard of bone might not get that far, I feel. I also remember that when kind neighbors gave my Irish some steak bones she had to go to the veterinarian because her intestines were packed tight with bone meal. Chewing on a veal knuckle is satisfying for a cat, and that is the limit to which I go.

Cats like to eat up on a table or counter rather than on the floor. Very little of Amber's life is spent on floor level. Leaping is the favored mode of locomotion. I feed Amber on one end of the long counter under the kitchen window and I eat at the other end. This means we both look out on the old well house and the wisteria and can watch the birds.

It has also led to some interesting discoveries as to taste in food. Amber is so fond of Petite Marmite that she must have a teaspoonful in a separate dish. If I have the lobster bisque, I either give her some or a wedge-shaped nose is in my soup spoon. If I have beef stew, she enjoys a portion, even to the onions and carrots. A little potato does no harm, she says.

She likes cheese so much that when I have a cheese sandwich she will go so far as to miaow unless her own sliver is ready.

And recently Amber decided, after all my worries

about vegetables in her diet, that she did like asparagus. I had by then given up the struggle with string beans, spinach soufflé and so on. But one time I fixed a dish of frozen asparagus for supper and the phone rang (it always does at mealtime). When I came back to the kitchen Amber was braced against the dish, eating asparagus tips as fast as possible. I praised her extravagantly and gave her all she could eat.

I couldn't remember that the experts recommended this particular vegetable, but it agreed with her very well. I went to the market and laid in a supply the next day. I found that having asparagus night after night got rather boring for me, especially since I had to eat the stalks while Amber consumed the tips. After two weeks, she decided she had had enough of that particular edible and went back to an occasional binge on mushrooms.

I haven't given up hope that she will change her mind about egg yolks, but so far her answer to egg is to draw back her velvet lips and walk away proud-legged. But I shall keep at it, remembering that even a kitten can change her mind.

Last week end my dear friend Olive brought me a jar of homemade cream of leek soup which I planned to have for lunch. Amber decided that was what she wanted for lunch also, and in the end, after assuring her she could not possibly like it, especially since it was well-seasoned, I gave in and put a spoonful in her dish. She actually seemed to breathe it in and came purring back for another round. At that point I decided that her diet was well-balanced in an odd way even if it did not exactly follow the lists provided by the experts.

Amber's silhouette became superb in adolescence.

I have heard the theory that cats never overeat, but judging by some cats I have known, this cannot be true. Country cats seldom do get too fat because they have so much exercise. Barn cats work for their living and generally live long and stay in good shape. But house cats sometimes are so fat they seem hardly able to move. Overfeeding shortens their lives, as it does with dogs.

As long as I can feel Amber's ribs, I shall not worry, but I do check on them every day or so to be sure she doesn't need to join a weight-watchers' club. Some days she wants more to eat, some days less, and her own system seems to balance it out very well so far. An Abyssinian seldom miaows at all, but occasionally she will leap to my desk, stare fixedly at me and utter that minute sound. It means she is absolutely starving and where is her dinner?

Usually it also means I have been working and forgot to notice the time, while her personal clock has been working. But now and then she decides in the middle of a late television show that she needs something. She gets it.

And one endearing thing about her is that every time she is fed, she jumps in my lap and thanks me with loud, persistent purring. Then she settles down on the desk and scrubs, even flattening her ears which never do get in her food.

One difference between dogs and cats is in the manner of eating. A cat uses her paws like hands, scooping up bits of food and putting them in her mouth. A dog uses his muzzle to push and arrange tidbits or shoves the whole dish around with his nose.

Once when Amber had a dreamy moment I examined

her paws. The four small parts tipped with pale rasp-
berry-colored cushions are prehensile, very like fingers.

"You've got an extra bend in them," I told her.

She purred and spread her toes apart with pleasure.

Her wrist is very flexible, more so than mine, I must
say. There is no thumb but I felt a small semipad tipped
with a flat claw. I think it is what we call a dewclaw
in dogs.

I read somewhere, probably in *The Territorial Im-
perative*, that it is the thumb which is largely respon-
sible for the difference between man and the other
mammals. This seems reasonable to me, since I once hit
my thumb with a hammer and decided a thumb was
basic.

When Amber sees me put down her food dish, she
advances on tiptoe, sniffing. If it is something she really
likes, she gulps and when she has finished goes over the
dish with a scouring pink tongue, sometimes putting one
paw inside to hold it still. If the food is chopped up,
she picks out the best morsels and carries them to the
corner of the counter, turning her back for privacy
while she holds them and pulverizes them. The less at-
tractive bits she pushes to the side with one paw.

She is fastidiously neat. If she spills a drop of anything, she cleans it up. When she is finished, she laps
a small amount of milk and then begins the eternal washing up, which she takes very seriously. It's important to
tidy up when the mealtime chores are done.

Chapter 7

My first experience in housebreaking a kitten was with Amber. Esmé and Tigger went outdoors when they needed to. Tigger would go to the back door, lie down, and roll over and over, which always worked. Esmé screamed. Occasionally in the coldest weather, Esmé used the toilet seat in one bathroom.

But Amber was to use her own pan since she could not go out in ten-below-zero weather. I was not worried since all of the books I read advised me housebreaking a cat was no problem at all. Generally the mother cat housetrains her kittens—and cats are naturally neat.

I had housebroken dozens of cockers, paper-training them. Most of ours were raised on *The New York Times* and the *Newtown Bee*. Now I had an elegant pale-green plastic rectangular pan with waterproof liners and a bag of kitty litter with a cleaning scoop.

I decided on my dressing room for the location since it was out of the way but near my room. The dressing room is nothing but the front entry on the east side.

There are five doors to the ancient house, and this one has never been used except for letting dogs and cats in and out. There is no path to it. It has room for a chest of drawers and one straight chair.

I knew a kitten couldn't be expected to run all over the house looking for a pan when the house must have seemed as large as a museum. It was quiet and dark in the dressing room; indeed it resembles a closet. I knew cats like privacy for the toilet.

The local Food Center carried the litter, so I could always get more. It smelled a little like cedar and was more absorbent than sand, and in any case I know how sand tracks around since I spend part of my time on Cape Cod. Most Cape floors look as if sandpaper had been rubbed into them.

As soon as Amber had her first meal, I took her to the pan and put her in it. A little later, I put her in again. Later I added some shredded newspaper since she had been used to that at the cattery. When a damp spot appeared, I scooped up the litter and put in fresh.

This worked perfectly as far as wetting was concerned.

However, Amber had never read a cat book and she had her own ideas about the rest of the bathroom business. Her first choice was at the foot of the stairs leading to the upper story. I felt it could scarcely have been a more unfortunate choice since people were always pounding up and down those stairs. I used some ammonia on the area, which took off all seven coats of Butcher's Wax.

Her next chosen location was at one end of the trestle table where nobody who sat down to eat could miss it. I took off some more wax and hoped for the best. Meanwhile I kept her in my room most of the time, feeling sure she would remember her pan because it was so nearby.

A few days passed and the pan got damp spots and that was all. Finally I discovered she had a fine secluded spot under the radiator behind the maple daybed. This old hot-water radiator has bookshelves built around it that go to the ceiling, and my business-office metal desk is at one end. To get under that radiator involves moving the daybed and the desk (both weigh tons). It then means lying flat on the floor and reaching in with soap and water. It took my agile teen-age friend Tommy to accomplish this feat.

While Tommy crawled under, he discovered she also liked the lower shelf of the bookcase—empty because inaccessible. The desk is in front of it. So the desk came out again. The cleaning job took, in all, two hours, and the kitten watched with interest, her head cocked.

"I don't want to do that again," said Tommy, shaking his red head.

So we tried to figure out how to close up the space. An old window screen was jammed in behind the desk, sealing off the bookshelves. Pieces of cardboard cartons went in and some old books were stuffed in the open end of the radiator.

Certainly a mature person should be able to outthink a small apricot kitten, I thought. I felt happy about everything until I decided to get back to work on the current book and discovered Amber had used the floor under the well of my desk as her newest bathroom.

At that point, I cleaned the floor again and spread

(Cape Cod Photos, Orleans, Mass.)

Amber enjoys TV (weather reports most) and Herb Alpert.

newspapers all over the surface and moved her pan from the dressing room to the fine cave under the desk well. And there it has stayed. This means that at regular intervals I stop typing and withdraw. Then Amber slips under the desk and turns her back and lifts her head high, staring at the top of the well. When she has finished her chores she leaps out and goes through the air like a jet plane, wild with triumph.

On the whole, I am satisfied. The pan and extra newspapers do not show, and they occupy what has never had anything but a wastebasket before. True, the wastebasket now sits in front of the daybed and is no object of art. It is a huge metal container I once painted smoky blue. It has rusted right through the paint. So I face the prospect of hunting in antique shops in the valley for an old sugar bucket to use for trash.

But I remember a woman I once met who had a cat that would only use the strings inside the grand piano for her toilet. So nobody could ever play the piano with the top up, and some musical works seem to demand an open top. And one cat I knew insisted on using the fireplace. This should have been cured by filling the pan with ashes, but the fireplace had more charm.

Most cats are more reasonable. Their own pan and some privacy is all they ask. If you do not have a special cat pan, a shallow pan from the hardware store will do very well. Plastic is easy to handle and to clean, but be sure to buy a shallow one. Cats like to see where they are. In case you cannot find the pan liners, plastic kitchen wrap will do.

The advantage of a liner is that you can lift the contents of the pan out all at once and dump it into the trash can. The pan stays clean, but if you want to wash it out, use only a mild soap. The smell of ammonia or carbolic acid will keep your cat away from the pan forever. The smell may make a cat actually ill, and this does not surprise me at all for I feel dizzy if I get near either one.

Once you have the pan located where you and the kitten agree is a satisfactory place, never change the location. You wouldn't like to hunt for a bathroom all over the house either!

Tay Hohoff disagrees with this as her own cat, Shadrach, will put up with having his pan moved when there are guests coming. She says he accepts it like a gentleman. I think she has a most unusual cat. Mine would never put up with it!

In general I feel any established pattern is easier for a cat. Amber does not even like a chair put in a different place. If I change the arrangement of milk glass on the harvest table, she approaches gingerly, then goes over each piece, inspecting it thoroughly and disapprovingly. A pile of laundry on the bed is stalked, examined, and finally accepted as good to nest in.

Although Esmé, Tigger, and Aladdin did not have pans, I think this was a serious mistake on our part. You cannot be sure you won't have a flat tire and be late getting home. In New England in winter there are a good many blizzards when even opening the door can be a problem. Or you may have an appointment with the doctor and expect to be in his office twenty minutes (hope does spring eternal) and sit two hours or more while the doctor is on an emergency call. Cats have a great deal of endurance and patience, but nature has a definite schedule. It is better to have a bathroom available at all times.

A small kitten may need to use the pan a dozen times a day, but the main bathroom business comes after the biggest meal. Amber flies to her pan at almost exactly four in the afternoon. She scratches up the paper with great vigor, following the basic tradition of cats. Afterward she races around the house leaping up and down and then works hard at her scratching post. And then naturally she washes herself from ear tip to tail.

Amber does have one rather odd reaction to her bathroom. She uses her pretty pastel pan with the fine kitty litter in it. But she uses it only for wetting. For the more serious business she steps carefully outside of the pan and nothing will persuade her this is not as good as using the pan for the whole affair!

We had to compromise after a prolonged struggle. I spread *The New York Times* all around the pan in thick layers topped with the smaller folds of *The Cape Codder* or *Newtown Bee*. She uses the newspaper and then scratches frantically, trying to bury everything neatly. After she has panted and heaved and clawed with discouraging results, I rescue her. And I may say she enjoys being rescued. She watches with interest as I pull out the necessary folds of paper, roll them up and slip a rubber band around the roll. Then she flies triumphantly about the house, waving her tail like a banner.

Actually this is easier than emptying the pan so often.

The whole problem of a cat's sanitation is relatively simple. It is not true, as some people think, that a house begins to smell of cat. If it does, the owner is failing to keep the cat clean and to empty the pan daily. If a kitten does make a mistake before she has settled down, a couple of tissues will clean it up. A damp sponge dipped in a mild detergent (no carbolic acid) will prevent a stain on the rug. I have been told that sprinkling salt on the spot will also fix it, but I have never tried this.

It turned out that Amber's original problems were due to the diarrhea from the intestinal infection she arrived with. It was always too far to the regular bathroom. But once the diarrhea was checked, that difficulty was over.

Chapter 8

There may be some stolid cats, but I have never known one. A cat has a naturally lively mind, and my life with Amber has kept me lively too. As for discipline and training—we have learned from each other.

Amber does not care too much for toys that are meant for cats, but sometimes in the night I hear her pouncing in the living room. If I am still up watching a late show, I investigate. I find she has been taking the cigarettes from the small pewter mug and tossing them all over the floor. Every cigarette is full of pin-sized holes.

I learned very soon to keep a cigarette on her counter so she could attack it.

She has also taught me to appreciate pencils. I like soft drawing pencils and so does she. She takes a newly sharpened one and knocks it to the floor, scoops it up, and tosses it and shoves it under the radiator where I cannot reach it. When I retrieve it with the dust mop, the point is gone and the whole pencil mangled.

She does have a few habits which some people might

consider need disciplining, but I am learning to accept them.

She enjoys doing over bouquets, especially roses. I keep a half-dozen sweetheart roses in my grandmother's silver teapot and spend some time arranging them just so. Amber watches, with her head cocked, and as soon as possible she takes the best rose and plays games with it. Next to chicken and roast beef and White Lilac perfume, rose is her favorite scent. She prefers it to catnip.

In a short time, petals are all over the floor and she is pouncing on the rose leaves. When I come in the room, she looks up with innocent eyes and with a rose petal under one paw. She indicates she likes roses and I explain that I do not know whether or not they would be a good thing in her small insides. Many house plants, I am told, are poisonous to cats. So I distract her with a small bit of chicken while I hastily sweep up the rose leaves.

The next thing I know she is inside the television set and I am terrified that she may be electrocuted. The television repairman told me terrible tales of this happening. I fish her out, complaining. Then I glue the television cord up on the bookcase with Scotch tape. (I wonder why they call it Scotch?)

As I have said earlier, one of her favorite sports is playing with water. I have learned to be careful about turning on the hot water. Lately she has become a flower-water addict too, so it is hard to keep flower vases filled. It is her theory that water tastes better if roses or daffodils are standing in it. In April she lowered the level in the forsythia pitcher until the pale gold flowers turned paler and paler. She can elongate her neck and somehow make her head slide around stems.

The vacuum cleaner is a delight for her, which is one of the few things we do not have in common. My hostility to the vacuum cleaner is no secret, but I think more kindly of mine since it means so much to Amber. That long snaky hose which trips me and winds around chair legs is a special treat to her. In the beginning, I wondered whether she might be sucked in by that hose, but she never was.

We have disagreed about one other thing. I cannot type when that golden head is in the key well and two deft paws are picking up the keys. It bothers my concentration and makes the keys knot up and stick. Also I have had to discourage her from unrolling the ribbon— I have trouble enough changing it even when that becomes absolutely necessary.

Then there is the matter of kitchen safety. The kitchen at Stillmeadow is U-shaped and the refrigerator, which goes almost to the ceiling, bisects one set of counters. I was happy about this when Amber came because it meant I had plenty of counter space inaccessible to her. The range was protected. And the counter under the window was free so that she could eat, play and doze in the sun there while I did kitchen chores.

But one night I got up to have a snack and turned on the kitchen lights. From the top of the refrigerator a small wedge-shaped face peered at me. The next minute she flew through the air and landed in the sink. From there it was easy to leap to the range.

No problem at all, she assured me.

(Cape Cod Photos, Orleans, Mass.)
Amber can look startled, but not ***much***.

Her feat was comparable to my leaping to the top of the two-hundred-year-old sugar maples. It was equally dangerous. I uttered my most anguished *No* and she vanished. But the next morning when I went out to plug in the coffee pot, a little golden face hung over the refrigerator top.

By standing on tiptoe, I reached her, and for the first time I spanked her. Now when I go into the kitchen, she flies from the refrigerator top and vanishes. But when I am safely in my room typing, I can hear the thud which means she has pushed the roll of aluminum foil from the top of the refrigerator. And by the time I run out, I find a beautiful Abyssinian tail waving in the sink.

This is probably good for my housekeeping because I cannot leave a single morsel of food on any counter in the kitchen and dishing-up goes at sixty miles an hour. Stacking the soiled plates is not feasible either, so they get washed immediately. I decided this when I found her eating broiled mushrooms that were on a breakfast plate. No cat expert ever said anything about mushrooms on a cat diet. How did I know they wouldn't poison her?

In fact, they agreed with her so well I wondered whether in the wild state cats ever nibble a mushroom on the way to a hunt.

Her games seldom cause me any bother.

When it comes to regular kitten toys, as I have said, Amber finds them dull. She cast a tentative paw over those she got for her first Christmas and settled for munching the ribbon and the tissue paper they came in. A paper grocery bag is better, according to her. She did enjoy taking ornaments from the Christmas tree, and I spent some sleepless hours wondering whether she had

86

really eaten any of those bangles and baubles or just hidden them in cracks in the old floor.

String, erasers, rubber bands, pens, bits of kindling from the wood basket and my best stockings are on the honor list. Crumpled balls of aluminum foil she often drags around, and a ripe olive lifted from the cocktail tray is delightful.

If all else fails, she scoops up a corner of the irreplace-able wool rug and builds a cave in it and chews off nubbins of wool. She also likes bed linen and I often hear Millie, the friend who comes to help me with the weekly household chores, advising her that this time she cannot punch holes in the sheets because these are the *good* ones! Next week, Millie promises, she will use the patched one and it will be all right. A few pillowcases have acquired frayed edges but are still usable, so I do not go into the No-No routine on those.

I have strong opinions on discipline. It should, I think, be sparing. If life is one long negative, nobody is benefited whether it be a child, a pet, or a husband or wife. Most of the problems of living might be solved if we emphasized only the essential.

Cats traditionally do not respond to commands as dogs easily do. I think perhaps the reason Amber obeys me when I say No is that I use it so seldom. If she is pulling the stuffing out of a shabby worn chair I keep quiet. If it is a chair covered with a documentary print, I firmly speak the word "No" as loudly as my rather light voice permits. She gives me an incredulous stare and rakes one last streak down the upholstery and then stops. In three minutes she forgives me and jumps in my lap.

Also, I am sure the reason she always comes when I

call her is that I only call her when it is necessary. Ninety per cent of the time when I worry about whether she has gotten stuck in a drawer or under the sink, I silently hunt. But if a strange dog is coming or unknown children (who invariably leave the door open), I call her. She has never failed to materialize from somewhere when I do call. She seems to know that this is not an idle exercise of authority but that it is important.

I admit it has been my theory as a dog raiser for years that much of the trouble owners have is their own doing. As my favorite reader once said, enough is too much of everything. Incessant repetition of commands, which is really nagging, works no better with animals than with humans.

My list of essential negatives for Amber has resulted in her paying attention to them. She knows she cannot slip into the refrigerator just because the door is open and I am getting out the lamb chops. She knows she cannot leap on the stove (although I always put a pan of water over a recently used burner, just in case). She knows she cannot rush out of the door when the groceryman comes in with a carton of groceries. And she knows she should not claw the newly upholstered sofa; when she hears this particular negative command, she flies over to her scratching post and claws at that, watching me with limpid innocent eyes.

One special characteristic of Amber's would melt the stones at Stonehenge. When I combine the No-No-No with a cuff (as when she chews the television wire), she might be expected to run away and hide. Instead she flies to me. Then we comfort each other! This certainly does not add to ease in discipline. I think a psychologist might say she feels I am her protector in time of trouble, and that I still am even when I myself cause the trouble.

This morning we had a new adventure. Over the fireplace on the Cape, two carved pale-gold-and-brown whales are silhouetted against a sea-gray background. They were copied by a gifted artist from a very old engraving. They each have two holes in the backs which fit supports about as big as broom handles in diameter and about two or three inches long.

It is a big fireplace and the whales are placed well above where a mantel would be if there were one. They are probably the most valuable pieces of art in the entire house, and seem to symbolize the whole mystery of the ocean as they swim forever on the imitation deep.

Early this morning for some reason Amber woke up and discovered the whales. They were not just decorations, they were creatures. Now the only fish she has ever seen is her own flounder fillet, which is headless, tailless, just a flat bit of pinky sweetness. But some deep instinct invaded her—the Abyssinian is said to have been the fishing cat of the Egyptians 4,000 years ago and who can know. . . .

I heard the sound and jumped out of bed, reaching the living room just as Amber landed on the right-hand whale, knocking it loose from one peg. Fortunately I just caught it before it crashed and cracked. Amber's leap was halfway to the ceiling from a flat take-off with no window sill or shelf as a help. The back of the whale she landed on is about ¼ inch thick and would not quite accommodate all of her.

She was preparing for another launch when I used a seldom-word very sharply. *No-No-No.* Then I started out to fix coffee and looked back to see her tensed on the chair top nearest the fireplace, gazing up with passion at the two somnolent whales. In the end, I added a small slap to the *No-No-No*.

I am grateful I do not have to say "No" often. It is upsetting to discipline a kitten and have her rush to you to be comforted immediately afterward.

Chapter 9

Grooming Amber was difficult at first because she wanted to play with the brush and comb. Her idea was to put both arms around the handle and wrestle with this odd gadget. It was a fine game, but her fur was only brushed in spots. She purred like a small motorboat.

Some experts advise a soft brush, and some a fine steel comb. I worried about this briefly and solved it by using both. So I had to be right half of the time. I can see that for a long-hair like an Angora or Persian, a comb would be advisable because the soft long hair mats so easily and a comb would make it possible to separate clumps, providing pussy went along with the idea. But Amber's coat is short and since she washes incessantly is pretty well polished. I sometimes get as many as three loose hairs with the comb. The brush gives an extra satiny gloss and that is about it.

And, of course, since I spend a good deal of time rubbing her, she is also hand-polished. A good many times in the day and night, she feels like being rubbed and leaps to my neck and begins nudging me and kneading her paws back and forth.

Dr. Whitney suggests that if your cat gets soiled, you can wet your hand and rub the body well, and the dirt and dead hair will cling to your hand. As of now, Amber has not fallen in the ashes or gotten in the trash basket, so I have never tried this.

Eventually she will get a bath. I know all the arguments against bathing both dogs and cats. Soap dries out the natural oils. It may cause irritated skin. The animal may catch cold. I am sure this is also true of human beings, but we manage to survive washing, and so have my own dogs and cats.

Even when we had thirty-five cockers, they had baths. Their coats were like silk velvet, their skins glowed. We washed them in the set tub in the back kitchen, which has a spray attachment fine for rinsing. The Irish setters were too heavy to lift into the tub, so they were washed with buckets of water in the yard, using a shampoo put out by a famous house and intended to preserve the natural oils in glamour girls' hair.

The dogs liked being bathed, but I cannot say the cats enjoyed it. Especially Esmé, the Siamese. We popped the cats in orange sacks and lowered them into the warm water gently. Then we rinsed them, still in the sacks, with the spray and wrapped warm bath towels around them. Esmé, although she objected strenuously, felt wonderful afterward. And if anyone who thinks bathing is wrong saw the color of the bath water, I could stop arguing.

As I reflect on this subject, it occurs to me that wild

(Cape Cod Photos, Orleans, Mass.)

Amber loves to be fed from a teaspoon.

animals get rained on and snowed on and run in the foggy foggy dew. Some of them go into brooks and ponds after prey. They run in wet fields or through damp high grass. They do not live in overheated houses where an endless battle with the vacuum cleaner goes on. Nature herself provides a soapless washing fairly often.

Probably primitive man got cleaned up too when caught in a driving rain far from the cave. And the women must have been soaked now and then when they went out for roots or berries or had to ford streams.

A cat's coat is naturally water-resistant, so if you don't want to use an expensive shampoo, one with a coconut-oil base is best as it penetrates the fur. There are many of these available. I have a lovely friend, a bank president's wife, who makes her own soap of bacon grease and lye, but I have never tried it! And she doesn't use it for the cat.

It is important never to let a cat get a chill, so warm bath towels are best for the drying process, followed by a good brushing. A cat's skin renews itself by sloughing off or scaling plus the hair shedding, and a good bath helps to remove the excess. It also helps if you have anyone with asthma in the house. Two members of my family lived comfortably with three cats even though the afflicted ones hung over a steam kettle in haying season.

Hair balls are often a problem with cats but not if the cats are kept clean. Long-hairs must be groomed with extra care because of the fine thick fur. A cat that has no help with this problem sometimes gets hair balls as big as a golf ball in the stomach or intestines, which may require surgery. Amber's close short hair sheds comparatively little.

The time-honored remedy for hair balls is vegetable oil added to the food. A teaspoonful of oil is enough for a kitten and a tablespoon for a grown cat. For a long-haired cat a teaspoonful once a week is a good precaution. Amber will not need it unless she begins to shed in midsummer. I do put a dab of butter on her dish, but if she did not happen to enjoy butter I would spread a dab of it on her paws, for anything on the paws gets licked off. A cat friend of mine prefers the oil from a tin of sardines, which tastes good and lubricates painlessly.

Ears are the most vulnerable part of a cat. Amber's ears stand up like wind-filled sails. When I noticed a waxy deposit in them and saw her scratch first one and then the other, I suspected ear canker or ear mites. Cleaning the ears with cotton swabs is better done by an expert since the ear is extremely sensitive and delicate. It does not take long. For a short time I dropped in some of the doctor's magic medicine and gently wiped out Amber's ears with a soft tissue. She enjoyed this immensely because ear mites cause an almost unbearable itch.

Once the condition was corrected, her ears acquired the delicate pinky glow which is characteristic. Occasionally I now wipe out her ears since they are natural dust catchers, particularly with Abyssinians who have especially large ears.

The care of teeth is simple. An adult cat has thirty teeth (we have thirty-two if we go regularly to the dentist). The enamel is thicker in a cat's teeth and the way they are set in the mouth discourages food particles from lodging between them. When Amber yawns, I can see the shearing teeth at the front, looking like minute ivory daggers. The inside of her mouth is seashell pink. This is the only time I can study it because she has an aversion to having her mouth opened except when she snips up her food or washes herself.

We used to take the cockers and Irish to the veterinarian once a year to have the tartar scraped off, but dogs' teeth resemble human teeth. As a cat grows older, it is advisable to check occasionally with the doctor, but if a cat gets some chewy food, such as pellets, bits of toast, or diced roast beef, there will be no problem. Bones are dangerous as they can splinter and rupture delicate tissues inside the cat.

When you pick up a cat for any purpose, whether for grooming, giving medication or just plain loving, there is only one way to do it. The mother cat picks her baby up by the scruff of the neck for just one reason, it is the only way she can. But a mother cat stops this as soon as the baby can get around by itself.

Small kittens, like puppies, should be picked up gently with one hand under the body to give a sense of firm support. I pick up Amber this way, and am always sure one hand is holding her hind feet. What is more important, I never dangle her in the air but hold her close to my chest. I can carry her all around the house in this manner, hold her to the window to wave good-by at departing guests, or show her the snowflakes falling outside. She purrs the entire time. But if a guest swoops her up so all four legs are hanging, Amber is plainly frightened and struggles to escape.

"Well, I can see Amber doesn't like me," says the guest.

I cannot say sharply, "Well, look at how you grabbed her, you idiot." On the other hand, I cannot say that Amber adores her since the evidence won't support this. But to assure the doubter that Amber really loves everyone but is shy does not solve the dilemma.

I am purely an amateur, knowing nothing about biology or any other ology, but as I watch Amber practically fly through the air, I try to think as she thinks. I decided that when she takes off from a dizzy height and levitates, she knows exactly where she will land and how firm the base is. The base is always solid. But if she is suddenly snatched up, she feels insecure.

Then too moving slowly and speaking softly is a basic rule for being popular with all animals. And with birds too, for the famous quail Robert, who was such a close friend of mine, was originally taken by the fact that I did not try to grab her, ruffle her feathers and make clucking noises. I kept as quiet as possible until she hopped on my shoulder and leaned against my neck.

Strange chirping noises or rattling keys or shrill whistling noises leave most animals and birds cold. They also immediately sense whether you really like them or not. This may have something to do with an acute sense of smell, for there is obviously an odor of fear which humans have in common with all mammals.

It may also be that people who are afraid of or reject animals make involuntary movements of withdrawal which we do not see but which animals perceive at once. It all boils down to the fact that you cannot fool a dog, a cat, or a bird!

When several people sit in front of the fire at Still-meadow, Amber may ignore those who are trying hardest to please and suddenly land with an enormous purr on the shoulder of one guest. She rubs her cheek against his or her neck, waves her tail, kneads her paws and tries to be as seductive as a movie starlet. But this is always a quiet guest.

It is generally better to keep a kitten away from small children if they have not had experience with animals. The one time Amber screamed was when a lively three-year-old grabbed her around the middle and squeezed as hard as she could, shrieking with excitement. Amber hid under the bed. My own granddaughters, Alice and Anne, happen to be exceptions to the rule since they have (I assume) inherited an empathy with animals as well as birds, butterflies, frogs, and so on.

Even very young children can be taught how to handle kittens or dogs. They should first watch how adults approach animals and rub the fur from head to tail—not backward—and how to pick up small animals gently and support the hind legs with one hand. Both cats and puppies feel nervous if there is no firm support for the back legs. Just dangling in air would not suit most people either!

My Irish setter, Holly, was a big dog and naturally loved children of any age. But she did not like to have her tail suddenly pulled with all the energy a small child could muster. Her reaction was a quick withdrawal from the scene.

Once children learn how to treat animals, a real affinity is established. And practically all children need to love a kitten or dog.

Chapter 10

I do not know who first said a cat has nine lives, but there are times when one fervently hopes it is true.

Another adage, "Experience is the best teacher," would, in my case, mean that I am now qualified to diagnose and treat a number of ailments. Most of the cats I have known have never had a sick day in their lives. Amber, however, is an exception. Together she and I have learned about a whole list of health problems (all of them quickly solved, I am happy to say). I know about gingivitis, for instance, because Amber had it. This is what happened. My beloved Cape veterinarian, Kim Schneider, was already examining her for some other minor ailment and opened her mouth.

"Well, well," he said in his light, comforting voice, "Amber has gingivitis, I see." And sure enough, all along the gums was a burning red line.

"Now you stop at the drugstore on your way home," said Kim, "and pick up a can of sodium perborate powder. Just make a paste of it and dip a bit of cotton in and hold it on the gums two seconds, then wipe it off with a clean damp bit of cotton. That's all you have to do."

I went to the drugstore and asked for the medication, and the clerk brought out a can holding about two quarts of powder.

"I only want it for a small kitten," I said weakly.

After thinking it over on the way home, I began to wonder if when people have gingivitis it takes two quarts to cure them. If so, I thought, I would never live long enough to cure Amber even with the small can the clerk finally found.

When we got home, I sat down and studied the directions on the label, and then waited for Margaret Stanger to come over and read them. The contents were to be kept away from children, it said in big print. Do not swallow. Dissolve one teaspoonful in a quart of warm water (this would make enough to drown a kitten). If inflammation sets in, discontinue treatment.

Margaret read the label three times.

"I thought you'd better come and help me," I said.

"Oh no!" exclaimed Margaret, "Suppose she swallows a drop or two?"

We discussed it, pro and con, for an hour and a half. How thick should the paste be? What if Amber choked?

Finally Margaret said, "I think we'd better take her back to Kim."

"You are a trained nurse," I pointed out, "and I have had years of experience with animals. We should be able to cope with a little adolescent kitten."

"I'll come over around ten tomorrow," Margaret announced, "and we will take her to Kim. We will just tell him we are chickenhearted."

(Cape Cod Photos, Orleans, Mass.)

Amber preparing to leap to my typewriter.

We turned up at the clinic at three minutes past ten, when the office opened. Kim did not seem surprised to see us, but in view of the times I have been there, I can understand why!

He took a Q-tip, rolled it in the powder and slid it along the gums so deftly that Amber did not even miaow. Then he used a small wad of cotton and rinsed the gums. The whole thing took only a moment.

"Now I think you two might manage this," he commented.

So I am now in a position to advise anyone who has a cat with gingivitis exactly how to proceed, for subsequently Margaret and I did manage very well. After all, a trained nurse and a kennel owner can certainly give medication to a kitten, as we told each other rather too frequently.

Be sure your kitten has the inoculations for enteritis, a deadly form of distemper which is no longer necessary in this day of modern medicine.

The most common ailment of cats and dogs is, of course, worms. Born and raised under the proper conditions, your newly acquired pet is not likely to have infestations of any of the various types of worm. But it is always well to check even so, whether you pick up a stray kitten or buy one from a mink-lined cage.

Roundworms are probably the most common, and a puppy or kitten can get them from the uterus of the mother. In short, Mamma passes them along to her offspring unless she is free from worms herself. Most reliable breeders check the brood matron before the babies are due—but don't count on it. The legend that milk causes worms is just that—a legend.

The symptoms are easy to spot. The kitten's belly seems bloated and there is a watery diarrhea. Sometimes the worms are coughed up, sometimes they appear in the stool. The breath has a strange sweet smell. The worms, when you see them, are like whitish rubber bands. If they persist, the coat becomes dry and thin and the kitten has no energy. (How could it when it is supporting a stomach full of enemy aliens?)

A veterinarian is the best help here as most of the patent medicines are not adequate. Garlic is thought to be a specific, if you use plenty of it, which is fine provided your kitten likes garlic. But a trip to the doctor is better.

Amber's first cleanup of roundworms was highly successful, but she had a recurrence later on and needed more medication. This time she threw up the green capsule, framing her mouth with foam. I called Kim, who assured me she would not die and had undoubtedly absorbed some of the medication before she threw it up. This must have been true for the worm problem was solved.

For comments on tapeworms, I have to go back to the dogs. Fish, raw, is a comfortable host for these parasites. Since Amber never has raw fish, this is no problem for her, but I have had dogs who brought home fine dead fish from the beach. Tapeworms, as I know, are easily identifiable for segments appear in the stool, looking rather like grains of rice. These worms are more difficult to eliminate than roundworms and cause vomiting, lack of energy, dull fur and, once again, a ballooning belly. The veterinarian can prescribe the necessary capsules and outline the treatment.

Fleas, which may also spread tapeworm, are a common

hazard. As you know if you have ever tried to catch them, fleas can hop very quickly. The eggs develop in the ground, but once you get fleas in the house they will flourish in cracks in the floor or in your kitten's blanket.

Most of the commercial flea powders are not safe for cats, who lick it all off. Derris powder is safe and may be mixed with 3 per cent rotenone and unmedicated talcum powder. DDT is fatal, and any product containing it may kill your cat in a hurry.

When using powder, be sure not to get it too close to the eyes or in the ears, but begin back of the neck and work it in carefully, including between the toes. My cats have never had fleas, but fleas are rare in my location, perhaps because they do not like twelve-below-zero nights in winter. Or perhaps because my pets have baths.

Ticks I have had plenty of experience with, although not with Amber. So far I have picked exactly one tick off her when we were walking in the yard on Cape Cod. It was wandering around hesitantly on her dense fur, as if it couldn't quite decide where to embed itself.

Actually ticks prefer dogs but will camp on anything from woodwork to kitchen towels if they have a chance. Most of them are bothersome but harmless, but there are those that carry spotted fever. When I am removing them, I never study them closely; an expert can identify the poison bringers but I can't. My definition of a tick is that it is the one thing that prevents Cape Cod from being Paradise itself.

The tick was originally imported to the Cape along with some Belgian hares or some kind of rabbit. However, it has now spread. There are ticks in the Rocky

Mountain areas which could not have come from Cape Cod; also there is the Lone Star tick which moves northward from Texas, and the brown tick which prefers to live in houses.

But I had lived in the Middle West, in Virginia and in New York City without ever realizing there was such a hideous creature as a tick. I found out when we came to Cape Cod with two cocker spaniels and an Irish setter. I was, then, in a state of euphoria because the Japanese beetles which were so thick in Connecticut were not evident on the shores of Mill Pond.

Then I learned about ticks. When we went back to Connecticut I spent the whole five-hour trip deticking the dogs so as to be sure we didn't import one to Connecticut. Others who crossed the bridge did not work so hard at it, however, so there are now ticks also in my part of Connecticut, although they are still rare.

Ticks bite through the skin and burrow into the body of the host. Then the tick body swells until it is like a small balloon. What fills it is the blood of your pet.

The best treatment for ticks is to get them off before they engorge. The procedure is a matter for endless argument as all experts have their own methods, many of which do not go along with mine. Mine has worked for some years. First I believe in catching the tick as soon as it gets on the animal. With cats or dogs who run free on Cape Cod, I check every time they come in the house. To be sure, it may seem difficult in the middle of a cocktail party to ask to be excused while you check your dog or cat for ticks. If you are with understanding friends, you sit on the floor and so do they and you all work at it. If not, excuse yourself and disappear with

Buff into a back room. In any case, you get those ticks off *before* they are embedded.

To remove them many people use tweezers and alcohol. You put a drop of alcohol on the tick, and when it feels the effect, use the tweezers. There are also various sprays, but I advise getting prescriptions from the veterinarian.

My own method has never failed. I seize as much of the tick as possible between my forefinger and thumb and twist it clockwise with a quick lifting motion. Then I drop it in a can of kerosene (I keep one ready during the tick season) and wash my hands thoroughly. I have a friend who also uses this method but holds the captured tick, flicks on a cigarette lighter and burns it up. Most people would get their hands burned up too, but she has a special gift.

If you do not twist the tick properly, you may leave half of it still imbedded in the animal. So for most owners, the alcohol method is safer. My method also involves getting them before they have set up house and home but are still on a rental basis.

A cat or dog who has not been deticked regularly may have a host of ticks. In that case a bath of Derris and soapsuds is indicated, using a proportion of one tablespoon of Derris to a gallon of warm water. Do not rinse off at once but pat the cat or dog with dry towels. Rinse the next morning and check again.

Ticks do not fly or run. They tend to hang on beach grass or in a wild stretch of meadow. When a cat or dog goes past, they drop on board. If your pet stays on mowed lawns, the danger is slight. But when I find a tick on a lamp shade, I wonder just what kind of immigration laws he followed!

Ticks are seasonal, but in recent years they seem to arrive earlier and stay later. I suspect they live all year long on rabbits. And I am not sure what part they play in nature's pattern, because few birds eat them and ticks do not eat other pests.

The cat's excessive cleanliness involves licking earnestly a good many times a day. This is the reason that cats develop hair balls, especially when they are shedding. Usually the cat will throw up a hair ball, but if it should move on to the intestines, only the veterinarian can save her.

Prevention is the best remedy. It takes only a few minutes to brush the fur daily. It is easy to put a dab of butter or a bit of oil on the paws. Many cats favor the taste of oil from a tin of sardines. Amber helps herself to the butter from the dish on the counter.

Ear mites affect both dogs and cats, as I have already said, but it bears repetition. Puppies and kittens from a commercial kennel or cattery are often well supplied with them. You can see a dark-chocolate waxy substance inside the ears and there is a sweetish odor, rather like stale cheese. The kitten shakes its head, rubs against furniture and is restless. The first treatment should be from the veterinarian because he can clean out the infection without damaging the delicate ear. He will give you an ointment to take home, which you can squeeze in gently yourself. Once you are rid of ear mites they are not likely to recur.

Skin infections sometimes occur too. If a kitten has

dermatitis—also called eczema—it may begin with a moist scab, generally under the front legs (at least in my experience, which is limited). At first you diagnose it cheerfully as the result of an insect bite. Then you notice that the kitten licks it constantly and the area is spreading. There appear a few raw places where a meticulous tongue has worked too hard.

A tube of salve from the veterinarian works magic. You just rub it in thoroughly so the kitten cannot lick it all off, and repeat as often as prescribed. Most kittens will run to you when they see that tube because this is one medication that feels so good they enjoy it. You need not worry about contracting the infection yourself.

When I first began treating Amber, I hid the tube and then nipped it out when she was on my lap. But I learned from her, as one should learn from one's cat. The surprise treatment upset her. When I started taking out the tube and telling her it was time and that the paste would really help the itching, she would sit quietly in my lap for the whole procedure. And then one day she poked at the tube cap with a tentative paw and waited for the paste to come out. And began to purr. I would like to have exhibited her to one of those people who believe cats are impossible to medicate.

The eyes of a cat are a special miracle. Cats do not actually see in the dark but they manage very well when there is not enough light for us to see by. Their pupils adjust according to the light rays. Cats also have a third eyelid in the lower part of the eye, which is a protection we do not have.

Usually all you need to do about your kitten's eyes is

wipe them occasionally with a soft tissue as sometimes a drop or two of fluid comes to the eyelid.

But when Amber began to look at me with only one eye, while the other was tightly shut, I got out the familiar carrying case and off we went to the veterinarian. Conjunctivitis is an eye infection easy to diagnose and simple to treat. A tiny squeeze of ointment once or twice a day clears it up. And the world looks better when you see it with both eyes wide open!

Sometimes a cat may get a weed seed or bit of sand in the eyes because of going through life hull down as it were. A bit of damp cotton may swab it out, but do not try human eyedrops unless the doctor says it is all right.

Mouth ulcers are often called rodent ulcers in the belief that cats get them from rats or mice. Kim Schneider has done a good deal of research on this, however, and says there is no truth in it. Cats raised in apartments where there is never a sign of a rodent have mouth ulcers as often as barn cats do. Amber had one, although she did not know a mouse from a handsaw at that time. The cause is unknown, says Kim firmly.

The cure is a treatment with pills. And a smooth easy-to-swallow diet. I used baby-food meats and the strained green beans with tidbits of minced chicken and beef and fish.

The diet was no problem. The pills were something else again.

When I myself have to take pills, they always stick crosswise in my throat, so I am not surprised it is hard for a dog or kitten to swallow them. The construction of a cat's throat makes it easy to choke on a foreign object.

I discovered that the best way to give pills is to mash them to a powder and mix them with something delicious.

Amber is very deft at sorting out small grains of something she doesn't like, but if pills are mashed very fine, she will eventually ingest them.

A capsule is a different matter, as I have indicated, and I would always go to my patient veterinarian to have it slipped in. He pinches the mouth open and holds the capsule with a pair of slender forceps. One lightning move and Amber is ready to wash her face. Fortunately most medication for cats comes in the form of pills or salves or smooth tasty liquids in tubes.

For example, the modern medication for constipation comes in a tube. You squeeze half an inch on the kitten's paws and it is rapidly licked off. When Amber developed this ailment, all I had to do was open the cap of the tube and she was beside me on the counter, waiting to have some of this marvelous stuff. She would gladly eat the whole contents of the tube and felt that a mere half inch was a very stingy portion!

It reminded me of the days when milk of magnesia went all over my Siamese, the floor and my dress. I can't stand the taste of milk of magnesia either. It is also about as easy to clean up as liquid cement.

The classic remedy for diarrhea used to be Kaopectate, but now mashed pills will do the trick.

Both constipation and diarrhea may come from many causes, but a change in diet often helps. For constipation strained baby food, green beans, a little olive oil, chicken broth and so on are advisable. For diarrhea omit vegetables and concentrate on protein.

(Cape Cod Photos, Orleans, Mass.)

Amber on my desk, more or less at rest.

If you have an outdoor cat with a private bathroom under the lilac bush you can still diagnose bowel ailments. Constipation makes the stomach hard and round as a golf ball. Diarrhea makes a cat thin from flanks to shoulders, and excessive eating does not bring any gain in weight.

Kidney disease may result from a number of causes, such as infections, injuries, or for no apparent reason. It is important to consult a veterinarian at once so curative treatment may be started early.

A loss of appetite and a constant thirst are warning signals. In chronic kidney disease the cat will be dehydrated and there will be a smell of urine on the breath.

Ice cubes, if the cat will lap them, help with the thirst and provide some water absorption. A low-protein diet is usually indicated, with cereals and fats and vegetables as a mainstay. (It is not easy to persuade your cat to do without meat and fish!) There is a special diet now available for cats with kidney ailments, which the veterinarian may advise. Half a can a day is sufficient for an adult cat.

A urinalysis is necessary and will have to be repeated until the veterinarian decides a return to normal diet is feasible. Modern antibiotics and penicillin are generally useful.

Kidney stones sometimes develop, which the veterinarian can detect by X ray. If a cat is in pain under his loins and runs a temperature and shows traces of blood in the urine or has diarrhea, a trip to the veterinarian is a must, and as soon as possible.

A not unusual ailment in some cats is bladder trouble, which is indicated by a male cat being unable to urinate or a female crying in pain. This is caused by an irritation from a kind of fine gravel. The veterinarian will take measures to reduce the inflammation and restore normal functioning in the bladder.

One ailment I have had no experience with is irritation of the anal glands. These are two small sacs at each side of the anus under the tail region. When a dog or cat grows older, these glands sometimes produce an excess of fluid which must be squeezed out. Some experts believe the glands are related to the musk glands of a skunk, but in any case, if a cat drags along the floor and bites the base of her tail it may indicate anal-gland secretion.

The cure for this is to press on both sides of the anal opening firmly with a piece of cotton, holding the tail up with your third hand. But I know one owner who has a regular appointment with the veterinarian instead, and I favor this myself.

Aside from eczema, ear mites, hair balls, and such, illnesses are rare in cats. With a minimum amount of care your kitten will be as rugged as the Pillars of Hercules. Occasionally, however, medical treatment may be needed. If you are near a veterinarian, this is not your problem; it is his. But if you live in the country, you may not want to drive miles to get to the doctor unless it is a case of life or death.

If you love your cat, you will sense at once when he or she is really sick. A cat's behavior is as readable as a book. But you should have a rectal thermometer on hand to check the temperature, before phoning the doctor.

An adult cat's temperature is 101.5 degrees Fahrenheit but can vary up or down a degree or so without being serious. If it is much above or below that, there is something wrong. Kittens may safely run a higher degree than an adult cat. To take the temperature, lift the tail and gently insert the thermometer, which you have greased with Vaseline, plain uncarbolated Vaseline.

Most cats do not mind this. In fact one time when Kim was taking Amber's temperature, the phone rang and he had a long conversation with a distracted owner while Amber stood patiently with the thermometer in her rear and I rubbed her ears.

A first-aid kit is a good idea, beginning with the thermometer and Vaseline. Then you should have gauze bandage rolls for compresses or whatever. Sterile cotton pads are always useful and rubbing alcohol for cleaning the thermometer or for dropping on ticks. A bottle of baby aspirin is helpful for easing pain or bringing temperatures down.

For my own kit I also have the miracle tubes of eye ointment, constipation medication and ear mite salve, just in case. If you are taking to the woods for a vacation, be sure to include a can of tomato juice in case your darling does decide to establish a beachhead by a skunk. Wash the cat in tomato juice after a skunk rendezvous. Cats, however, are much less likely to get in trouble with skunks and porcupines than are dogs. As for snakes, cats do occasionally kill them. This is not a problem in New England, but it may be in areas that abound with poisonous snakes. If you live in snake country, you should keep snake serum on hand and ask your veterinarian how much to give your cat.

A swelling with two small punctures indicates the location of the snake bite. You inject the serum, and while you wait for the veterinarian, cut the swelling with a razor blade and squeeze out the poison. Keep warm water running over the area—someone in the family can hold a teakettle over it and keep pouring.

I am told cats take care of a great many poisonous snakes, so they must have been natural enemies in the dawn of history. My cats have never killed so much as a grass snake. We did have one blonde cocker who brought them in, but the cats never did. Amber has never even seen one and wouldn't know what to do except swell up and hiss.

After all this about cat health, I am reminded of a nervous friend of mine who has raised a block-busting family of boys and whose husband could qualify for a quarterback. But she keeps a medical dictionary on hand and if anyone coughs, immediately looks up lung cancer. It is not necessary to suspect your cat of lethal ailments or Excedrin headaches. Most kittens and cats are as healthy as anything on this planet. They have a natural stamina which I envy and a will to survive that front-line soldiers possess.

Chapter 11

That ancient Egyptian cat goddess was, among other things, the fertility deity. Since the country is overrun with homeless cats and Animal Rescue Shelters are full of abandoned kittens, it is obvious that female cats still produce litters with impressive regularity. The number of kittens varies from cat to cat and breed to breed. The Abyssinian usually has only two, but country cats have more. I have heard of one cat who had three hundred kittens during her lifetime.

Of course there was the case of Josephine, who belonged to some friends. When they decided it was time to have kittens, they invited a male cat to the house. A major battle ensued. Josephine was a beautiful cat, so they did not give up. They entertained another male. Josephine nearly lost an ear. On the third try, the visitor retired bloody and bowed.

They decided to consult the veterinarian: why did Josephine refuse to have kittens?

"I can tell you one reason," he said. "This is a male cat."

So they went sadly home with Joseph.

If Joseph had been a female, she might have come in season as early as six months. The average male is ready to mate at about eleven months. But it is not possible to mark a calendar for cats, as you usually can for dogs, because their times of season vary. Some males are mature at around six months, some not until a year and a half. Amber, at ten months, still showed no interest in sex.

The question of whether to spay a female or neuter a male is a difficult one to answer. If you own a female who comes in season regularly you can let her run loose the rest of the time. One litter a year is enough if you care about the cat herself, and when she comes in heat and is not bred, the caterwauling begins.

The male in heat sprays the furniture and also caterwauls. If he can go out at will, he will find a mate somehow, but if he cannot, the house will smell like a subway toilet.

Amber first came in season when she was exactly a year old. I had planned to board her when necessary but decided to put it off as long as possible, and she agreed with me that we were happier together no matter what. Fortunately we were on Cape Cod where all our visitors, from the milkman to the gentle neighbors down the road, are very careful about standing in the open door to talk. Also we do not have five male country cats regularly patrolling the yard, as we always have at Stillmeadow.

There are dozens and dozens of rabbits who are only interested in eating my best Peace roses. And plenty of hoppety-hopping quail that expect you will not run over them. But cats are scarce.

So we decided to stick it out at home.

Amber began by rolling on the beige rug and digging her claws in, then adopting the stance of a lioness about to pounce, switching her tail as rapidly as a flag in a nor'easter. The second day she discovered new vocal cords, and my whisper-soft miaower uttered a sound that made me drop Kennan's *Memoirs* and run to rescue her. But I could not rescue her from nature!

The sound began deep in her small throat and progressed to high C, reminding me of an opera diva in Act III. Her eyes were deep and big as jungle pools. When I picked her up to offer futile comfort, she trembled, but was much too involved to give me the usual sandpaper kisses. I put her down, and she ran the length of the house, leaping halfway up the living-room drapes.

Now all this is *not* easy, but I discovered one thing that none of the experts I knew of had mentioned: the hyperactivity is not incessant. After the first seizure, Amber retired to my bed and dozed. When she woke up, she slipped into my workroom and took part of my typewriter ribbon off as usual.

The spells of course recurred, but we felt we could manage.

The first two days she did not care much about food, but she did consent to eat from a teaspoon. A good many cats I have known would benefit from a brief period of dieting, but since Amber barely managed to make five pounds on her birthday, I fed her with the teaspoon.

The season lasted five days, and during the entire time she never kept me up at night. The only problem was that she was in a moaning spell when someone came to interview me for a feature article, and they decided, I knew, that I had a dying kitten on my hands. I shut Amber in the bedroom, and the sound was diminished enough so we could talk above it.

My conclusion was that Amber was better off being able to race through her own house than to be shut in a small cage, with the added misery of being away from home. The inconvenience of the sobbing fits was not too much to bear.

At the risk of being called sentimental, I must say I was better off too for being able to offer some small comfort and enabling her to go through this experience without adding rejection to it.

Any relationship between living beings has times of trial, but the soundest involve sharing the difficult times as well as the easy. And when her season ended and Amber jumped on the typewriter keys and started the usual purring and put out a raspberry-pink tongue to kiss my hand, I felt that she subconsciously was grateful that I had not put her away when she was miserable!

In this day of new medications there are pills which will help during the main season, but since cats are so sensitive to medicine, I have not tried this. I have heard of cats who died when the owners gave them sedative pills at this time, and I feel the risk is too great just to save oneself a short period of inconvenience.

The exception to this is when a cat comes in season every month or so. I have a friend with such a cat, and in this instance heartily advised spaying.

No cat should be altered before eight months of age, and no female bred before the second season. As far as neutering a male is concerned, it is not a serious operation and the cat can come home the same day.

Spaying the female cat costs from twenty to forty dollars. The cat must be perfectly healthy and have a thorough medical check-up first. For a male, since the operation is simpler, it is less costly. The price runs from ten to twenty-five dollars. One advantage in sterilizing a male is that he no longer engages in battles and comes home with torn and bleeding ears. He also is less likely to wander so far as to be lost. He should be at least eight months old before being altered.

But with a female the operation is not so simple.

Spaying the female requires cutting the abdomen open and taking out the ovaries and means a stay in the hospital to allow healing. This is nothing to be under-taken casually. Sometimes there is an emotional change in the cat, and a lovely, affectionate, lively companion may become cranky or eccentric or lethargic.

My own feeling is that if it isn't possible to keep a female confined while in season, a few days at the veterinarian's is far better than having that operation. The time is from four to seven days, and it seems to me preferable to cope with those days than run the risk of a major operation.

Our male cat, Tigger, spent a lot of time outdoors with lady friends at certain times, and since he was a most beautiful satin-black Manx, the kittens he sired were always welcome. Even now I sometimes see a handsome bullet-headed ebony cat dozing in a bed of violets on Jeremy Swamp Road, and I know this is a grandson or great-grandson of Tigger.

If you have a female and decide that a batch of gay fuzzy kittens would be an addition to the family, you may find a suitable male. Most veterinarians advise a

Amber helps with the mail.

second breeding a day later to be sure of a pregnancy.

The kittens usually arrive in sixty-five days, although the pregnancy may last for as long as seventy-one days. The prospective mother cat will behave as usual until the last week, but must be fed added calcium to prepare for the kittens to come. This is a good time for vitamin supplements and extra tidbits. When the cat begins to pace around, it is also time to fix up the nursery so she feels at home in it. A big carton is the best. (What would we do without cartons?) You cut a door in one side, leaving enough of a sill to keep the babies from crawling out. Torn newspapers make the best lining, so the mother can push them around, and when she has the nest to suit her, you can lay a baby blanket over the papers, plus a towel which can be taken out and washed.

When the kittens are born, a hot-water bottle wrapped in a soft towel is a help to keep the newborn babies warm until the whole family is settled in. As each kitten arrives, tuck it in the box, close to the hot-water bottle, while the mother is bearing the next one.

The mother cat usually cuts the umbilical cord herself, but if she fails to do so, you can cut it for her with blunt scissors, but be careful to cut about an inch and a half away from the body. Occasionally a nervous mother cuts it too close, and a hernia is the result.

There must be an afterbirth from every kitten, and if it does not come you may draw it out, if you are a courageous and deft person. Otherwise I hope your veterinarian can make a hurry-up house call.

Of course you may also take your cat to him beforehand, especially if it is a first litter and you have already promised a kitten to certain worthy friends. But the security of being at home is worth a great deal to your cat, and you will personally benefit by being present to help with the miracle of birth.

When I think of the homeless alley cats who find a damp cellar-hole and have their kittens in a pile of debris, I wonder once more at the mysterious stamina of nature. These kittens will be nourished by a semistarving mother, and survive to hunt garbage tidbits. They will have one heritage, the will to live.

So it is with the huddled masses in the ghettos. In a country with an oversupply of food, it is increasingly hard to understand why the innocent and helpless cannot be fed and sheltered. But the experts are not solving this problem very quickly!

Now back to your privileged kittens. They should be weaned by eight weeks of age. If the litter is too big for the mother to manage well, you may give supplementary feedings to the smallest ones before weaning, and if so, you need a formula. An easy one consists of 1 cup of whole homogenized milk, 1 egg yolk, 1 teaspoon of dextrose, 1 teaspoon of lime water. Or you may get a special preparation from your veterinarian.

You can feed this by a nursing bottle, at room temperature or a bit warmer. Use a doll's nursing bottle if the kitten is very small. The kitten will take about a teaspoonful or a bit more five times a day. You will know he has had enough when milky bubbles foam around the mouth. After feeding, if the mother cannot give the kitten a rubdown, you will have to do so. This encourages circulation and elimination.

By the time the kittens are twelve days old, their eyes will open, but they should not be exposed to strong light until they are about a month old. If the lids are gummy, you rub them gently with damp warm cotton followed by a rub with dry cotton.

When the kittens are old enough to be on their own, you will have a difficult time letting any of them go. But if you cannot keep them all, you can use selective judgment as to who carries them off.

Perhaps Mr. and Mrs. Brown turn up with two small children. The Browns couldn't care less about a pet, but the children have nagged. One child grabs a kitten, squeezes it, hauls on the morsel of tail, makes loud noises and tosses it in the air while the parents talk about the current heat wave. This bodes ill for the kitten. The main care will be left to the parents who are *not* interested. The obstreperous child is not going to be trained. The Browns will soon report the kitten is nervous and hides under beds all the time and won't eat the catfood. Also, she scratched the boy when he wanted to play games with her.

Another couple turns up because Mrs. Abbot is dying for a kitten. Mr. A. says cats are all right in their places but no cat is going to claw the furniture in *his* house.

A third family sits quietly while the children drop down to kitty's level and gently reach out small damp hands. The father wants to know exactly what kind of diet is best, and the mother asks if extra inoculations are necessary. They go off with the best kitten in the litter, while the Browns and Abbots remain catless as far as you are concerned.

By the time the kittens go to new homes, the mother cat is ready to rest, for she works hard rearing the babies. I have heard of only one cat who struggled against being bred and was forcibly bred anyway. When the kittens were due, she slipped out of the house and bore them in an old iron kettle half full of water. I feel convinced that in some mysterious way (who can ever really understand nature?) she knew these kittens were not normal, so she drowned them at birth.

We once had a cocker puppy born with a cleft palate, and the mother at once pushed that puppy to the corner of the nursery before we even discovered it. Just how she knew something was wrong is another of nature's mysteries.

When you part with a kitten, send along a favorite toy and a finger terry towel that smells of home. After all, when we go to strange places we take a suitcase full of familiar belongings. I have one friend who even takes her own soap when she goes traveling. If the kitten is used to one brand of kitty litter, send a bag of that along too. Also give the new owners a card with the diet list.

I am reminded of Margaret Stanger's supermarket story. She stood between two men, both with carts full. The first cart was piled with a dozen varieties of catfood.

"I am returning it," said the harassed man. "She can't decide which brand she likes best."

"Well," said the second man, waving at his cart, "I've got a dozen cans of nothing but tuna here. Mine has changed her mind about the brand!"

Cat lovers admit that a dog will eat anything, right or wrong, but that a cat is likely to starve unless the food is to her taste. So I imagine that even alley cats pick over the garbage and only consume what seems best to them. In any case, a kitten will settle down more quickly in a new home if the first supper is a favorite food.

Chapter 12

Amber is a private person. This seems contradictory when I think about how she helps the workmen who come to keep the house together. I decided when I first had her that she was the whole world's intimate friend. But when the summer guests began to arrive I found I was wrong.

Because of our experience, I would never advise anybody to try to show off a kitten or a cat. I had very beloved guests coming and had given them glowing descriptions of Amber's charms. So gay, so affectionate, so warm and so on, for two pages in my letter.

The meeting was a disaster. Amber took one look and hid under the sofa. After an hour or so, she emerged and skittered to the bedroom and got under the bed.

"Timid, isn't she?" said one of the visitors.

After another half hour, the small apricot face appeared in the doorway and Amber flew to a window sill and crouched behind the draperies. Her hair was literally standing on end.

"Does she *ever* let you pet her?" asked my friend.

I made the mistake of reaching out a hand, and Amber flew past me to the bedroom again, as if she had never seen me before.

There was not much to say so I said nothing. A few days later this friend admitted she thought cats were all right in their place but she turned cold when one came near her. This friend would gladly lay down her life for a dog but has *that feeling* about cats.

The next day a couple came in and sat visiting. Amber tiptoed out and began to sniff the gentleman's shoe and he put one hand down and she rubbed against it, purring her jet purr. She ignored his wife, who was also a cat lover and had lived with cats all her life.

"What a lovely affectionate cat," said the man.

His wife looked hurt. Amber never even went to that side of the room, but spent her entire time making up to the lovely man.

It is the same situation when small children come. Amber chooses one and follows that one around, purring happily. The others send her to the haven under the bed.

I no longer explain to guests that Amber wakes me up in the morning by purring lustily in my ear and sandpapering my face with that rough small tongue and then rolls over, spreading her toes in happiness because I have finally come to life, even groggily. I do not mention how hard it is to write a letter with a cat sitting on the paper, or to wash dishes with a small nose hanging over the dishpan, or to be sure the shower water is not too hot when she gets in the shower with me.

Typing may not be easy when a cat is sitting on the keys, but it is not lonely. When someone doubtfully asks me if Amber is companionable, I simply say that she is!

People who do not understand cats are not going to understand anything about them, and people who do never need ask.

But everywhere I walk, I have to be careful not to step on that five pounds of mobility. When I sit down, I look where I sit in case she is there before me and I might squash her. And I have to be prepared to stop anything and hold her and cherish her because suddenly she feels lonely. If I happen to be cooking, I turn off the stove and tuck her under my chin and rub her ears and assure her that I still love her just as much as I did an hour ago.

When she feels perfectly secure, she jumps down and chases a moth or swings on the Venetian-blind cords once more. And I turn on the stove again and hope what I am cooking will turn out all right.

Analyzing a cat's reactions is probably like doing an endless puzzle, but I can never stop working at it, because it is so fascinating.

I *think* the reason Amber loves workmen so much is that they are busy doing interesting things and never attempt to invade her personality. She can pounce on a discarded washer or a bit of rubber tubing, and when they reach over to pet her, it is in a casual way. I *think* that with strangers who come in and sit down, she is self-conscious. And if they jiggle keys or dangle the catnip mouse in the air, she is not sure what their motive is.

She definitely does not like to be swooped up by a stranger. But she loves Faith Baldwin and Margaret Stanger and Millie.

There is one final thought about people-cat relationships. Nothing in life is static as far as I know. Even the giant blue boulder on the beach at the Cape has changed subtly in the years I have been its friend. Impact of wind and storm and ice widens the fissures, smooths the rough places. My relationship with Amber grows deeper and richer as we face the vicissitudes of life together (which may be a cliché expression but which fits). She understands more of my curious human ways and I now know what she tries to communicate. Every day we make new discoveries. Also I observe my cat-phobic friend reaching out a hand to rub Amber's ears and just happening to find the catnip mouse to pull along the floor!

Last week a friend said to me that I ought to live my own life. Why not board Amber and take a few trips? Why should I be so tied down? I thought about it on the way home. I had been away about two hours, and as I drove up to the house, a small figure was perched on the nearest window sill and a lonely voice uttered a faint miaow. The expression in those two golden eyes would have done credit to a tragedienne.

Now I knew very well that Amber had been dozing comfortably on her pillow all the time I was gone until she heard the car motor. But when I went in, she dashed across the floor, giving a last desolate cry before the purr motor went on. She had, she intimated, suffered intensely and why did I abandon her?

Ten minutes later she was chasing a moth and definitely leading *her* own life!

So I sat down and watched her leaping incredibly high in the air and thought about people and pets. For many people, a pet is something to have around, to feed and keep in good health but something which is never, under any circumstances, to interfere with any plans of the owner. That is, to me, a pretty one-sided relationship.

It is one quite foreign to me. I feel a responsibility to the living being who shares my life. I do not consider Amber as a toy to be discarded at times, then picked up again. I have always longed to go to Greece, but I think that when I looked at the Parthenon, I would see in the midst of that magnificence a small apricot-colored cat pressed against the bars of her cage, left behind in a world she could not understand.

After all, nobody makes you have a pet. If you cannot bear to leave a dinner party early in order to be home at a decent hour, you do not have to own a pet at all. To own and be owned by a pet is one of the few voluntary occupations left in this atomic age.

As for me, as I write this, I feel rewarded because I suddenly have to write with one finger since there is a beautiful kitten with her paws on the keys and purring madly because we are together. Who needs the Parthenon?

Chapter 13

Since Amber is so exquisite, she is photographed nearly as much as a starlet. This has taught me a lot about the best way to take pictures of a cat. Our last experience was especially difficult. A fine professional photographer came from Worcester to take color pictures for a feature article.

As he walked in, past the sign PLEASE DO NOT LET THE CAT OUT OF THE DOOR, he saw Amber, a golden silhouette against the background of Mill Pond (this was on Cape Cod).

"Who is the kitten?" he asked, unslinging a camera.

"My Abyssinian."

"I never saw one like that!"

"Well, it is a rare breed."

Photographers remind me of Alpine climbers; they carry almost as much gear. This one was tall, rugged and handsome and did indeed look as if a few Alps would be no problem.

"I'll just take a few shots of her," he said happily. "Is she friendly?"

Amber went right over to him when she heard his soft musical voice, and she reached out one apricot paw to touch his moccasin. It was, once more, love at first sight. However, it was unfortunate that she was having a relapse from her first heat and by the time he had the camera ready, she was rolling on the floor and moaning. Hoping for the best, I picked her up. This outraged her. She landed back on the rug and rolled and sobbed. Even lying down himself, my friend could not focus on anything but a cat in torment.

As he said after two hours, all a photographer needs is patience. My own gave out after I had chased Amber all around the room, offered countless tidbits of chicken, blown the soundless whistle and tossed the catnip mouse. I used half a box of tissue mopping my face.

"Let's try her on the typewriter," he suggested. "I hear she sits on it when you work."

I laid bits of chicken on the carriage. Amber scooped them up instantly and was off like a jet. I finally got her back and held her.

"Could you hold her a bit *easier?*" he asked.

"If I don't squash her, she won't be here," I told him.

Meanwhile Millie, my beloved neighbor, had dashed out to pick the last of the pink roses and had arranged them in grandmother's silver teapot on the Shaker stand by the fireplace thinking the photographer would want to take a romantic picture of the author sitting in the armchair.

Not at all. What he wanted was a picture of Amber

(Cape Cod Photos, Orleans, Mass.)

Amber cares more about today than days to come.

in her harness, posed on the top step going down to Mill Pond, with the sea in the background.

But Amber flung herself down and rolled and got her small face covered with dead grass.

"I wish I could stay all day and take pictures of Amber," he said regretfully, "but I have to go to Provincetown to photograph the Pulitzer Prize-winning poet."

As he left I sat down. So did Amber. She was all over her relapse and in the next hour assumed one elegant pose after another—on top of the sofa, on the chair by the roses, on the window ledge overlooking the sea, and playing leaping games with a pencil she took from my desk.

"All I hope," I said to Millie, "is that the poor man doesn't find that poet has a cat!"

Even under normal circumstances, I think the best way to photograph a cat is to keep the loaded camera ready and not pay any obvious attention to the model. Then you might be quick enough, if you make no sound, to take a snap of the kitten busily scrubbing her paws and scouring her ears. You might catch her peering out of a blue sheet in the unmade bed, provided she doesn't know you have that little black box anywhere near.

You might even catch her leaping after a moth or looking down from the high shelf where the Balleek plates are displayed.

A movie camera would be even better. Cats are full of surprises. As I have said before, the typical image of a cat dozing by the fire isn't exactly a true one. Perhaps the typical image of a horse galloping wildly isn't true either, for I imagine horses do stand around sometimes!

Amber may sit by the fire briefly, but the next thing I know she is clinging to the top of the family-room window, chittering away at a squirrel who is eating something too near the house.

Her acrobatics at Stillmeadow are spectacular. The windows are twelve-over-eight small panes and the dividers between the panes are narrow. Somehow Amber keeps a precarious toe hold with her front paws and manages to put one hind foot on a lower divider. The leftover paw swings loose in mid-air. A tightrope walker would envy her balance. And I would love to have it all on film.

She herself now seems inclined toward literature. Since I began writing about her, she has watched the typewriter with fixed attention. As I have noted, in the beginning she jumped up and down on it whenever she had a chance, with sometimes disastrous results. As of now she types in the same manner as I do, tapping the keys lightly and staring at the carriage. When she hits the space bar she bounces with pleasure. She no longer tries to catch the ribbon or chew the keys as they pop up. In fact, her only problem is that she cannot as yet spell as well as I can.

Chapter 14

Amber and I have lived together for a year and a month as I write. I cannot imagine the house without her. On those dark days we all have, I may sit gloomily staring into space. But not for long. Amber skims in with a small ball of aluminum foil which has become a treasure. She tosses it in the air with one swift paw, pounces, withdraws and stalks it, loses it under the bureau and flattens herself as she pokes it out. Her intensity is something to envy. Few of us devote ourselves so whole-heartedly to any project. And always when I watch her, the darkness brightens.

Sometimes she takes a pencil from my desk and chases it all over the house. What I admire most is that the pencil, which really hasn't much life of its own, suddenly takes on a personality—she is being the fugitive pencil as she is also the pursuer. When she is tired of it and I pick it up from the back kitchen floor, I really expect it to jump in my hand. But for me it is lifeless and all I can do is sharpen it.

The house itself has changed since Amber came into

it. Almost all of the drawers are ajar so that if she slips in she can get out again. And since the day I opened a kitchen cupboard and found a worried Abyssinian in with the pots and pans, I keep that cupboard door partly open.

In fact if I do not see her for twenty minutes, I hunt for her. A cocker spaniel or an Irish setter is always visible, but a small cat may be inside the television set or on top of the refrigerator. Cartons and brown paper bags must be carefully examined. I once almost put Amber out for the trash man. When a large grocery bag began to vibrate, I realized my mistake.

When people ask me whether it is better to have a cat or a dog, I always say, "Both." Each in its individual way enriches life. They give you more than you can ever give them. My own idea of happiness involves two or three cockers, two Irish, three cats. When I see advertisements for Cartier's eight- and ten-thousand-dollar pieces of jewelry, I realize anew that I would prefer one small kitten and one bouncy puppy to any amount of diamonds and sapphires to pin on my bosom.

However, I realize that if you live in a city apartment or in a house near a throughway, you face limitations other than noise, dirt and polluted air. We did have several cockers in a New York City apartment in the past and managed one litter of six who were born under the sofa despite our efforts to persuade the mother that the linen closet was all set up for her whelping.

But I would not advise this procedure for anyone less besotted. The grown cockers went out four times a day on the leash. I spent more hours toiling through Central Park than any athlete puts in when training. During blizzards or hurricanes the dogs used their paper bathroom, but this did not provide the necessary exercise. Of course very small breeds do not require as much exercise, but even miniature schnauzers do need to go out of doors every day.

No matter what your city schedule is, you always have in the back of your mind a nonelectric clock measuring the time you have to spare before you must get back to take Honey for a walk. If I ever got home late when we lived in the city, the ancient elevator man Albert would hold the elevator for me until I scrambled back out with my dog. At such times he steadfastly ignored all pushed buttons on the other six floors and creaked us down as fast as possible. Fortunately, we moved to the country and fenced in a quarter of an acre, and this problem was settled.

A normal kitten gets enough exercise in the apartment or house. A dog does not leap to the top of the window, then skim to the chest of drawers in the bedroom and aviate to the back kitchen counter. Amber exercises madly until she finally folds up in a relaxed furry ball on the top of my typewriter. In good weather when she goes out with her harness on, she enjoys eating a certain kind of grass, chasing ants and moths, and smelling the roses. But when she has to stay in, she is not underprivileged.

From this point of view, I would consider a cat better for confined living. Also, the people in the next apartment can never complain that they hear barking in the middle of the night.

If you live outside of the city in a reasonably uncrowded suburb, you may not have the exercise problem even with dogs. In that case, a dog may head your Christmas list. If there are small children in the family, a puppy has advantages. A puppy will play any time the children feel like playing; a kitten plays only when she herself feels like it. Also, a puppy will endure a lot of rib squeezing which a kitten cannot abide.

A dog will do almost anything to bolster your ego, but a cat is interested in her own and not yours. I notice with Amber that even some of my adult friends have their feelings hurt if they want to dangle a string and play games when Amber is through with games for the time being and impolitely yawns in their faces.

"All right if you don't care," they will say.

Amber and I have no problems of this kind. When she feels like playing, I stop whatever I am doing and we play. When she wants to tuck up on a pillow, I never urge her to chase a toy mouse. If I am in the middle of a manuscript and she feels lonesome, she leaps on the desk and scatters the pages until I stop and gather her up and rub her ears and smooth the downy apricot underchin and utter those sentimental words only another cat lover would understand.

Since I believe many of us live too much by routine, I find this arrangement very satisfactory. Too often we feel we must organize every minute. Time dominates us and we find we are very tired. If every day is regimented, tension builds up.

Now that Amber manages our schedule, I have given up dividing the day into hours and half hours of chores and work. I seldom look at the clock to be sure I am on schedule for I know that I shall not be. Perhaps I have lost a half hour in the middle of the day when

Amber decided to take a nap in my lap. How could I disturb her? Sometimes at night I miss a favorite television show because I cannot get up to turn it on without interrupting her exquisite sleeping form.

But I can always watch how she tucks her paws under her delicate chin and folds the slim tail completely around her downy self and feel the quick small heartbeat under my hand. I hear the soft throb of that mysterious purr, and put one finger on her throat to try to discover just where it comes from. Then when she opens her topaz eyes and looks long and deeply at me and increases the vibration of the purr, I feel a sense of wonder beyond description.

Sharing life with Amber grows more rewarding daily, for there are fringe benefits from the sharing. Now I know when she walks with a certain rolling gait it means she wants breakfast but is in a mood to have me feed it to her in a teaspoon. A pale, barely audible miaow indicates that it is ten minutes of ten and I ought to get up and visit with her. If I have been up until one thirty and do not leap out of bed at her suggestion, she starts scrubbing my face (don't we always wash in the morning?) and paddling spread paws on my neck.

Most of life we spend trying to understand someone or something and often never are able to communicate. But with dogs and cats and other animals and some birds establishing communion seems easy. Amber listens attentively to everything I say.

It goes like this: "I have to get the mail now. I won't be gone any longer than I can help."

Amber makes any sea- or landscape look better.

Amber is already in the kitchen window ready to watch me drive off, and looking so desolate I almost decide to let the mail go!

This cannot be explained because of a time pattern for I seldom go for the mail at the same time. When I go out to dinner, I explain how long I shall be gone. She listens mournfully and then goes to the living-room picture window and sits on the sill.

If I tell her we shall go for a *w-a-l-k* as soon as I finish a page more at the typewriter, she jumps from my lap and leaps to the trestle table by the front door and waits.

It is fortunate I never try to deceive her for the candid steady gaze of her eyes would penetrate any trickery. For this reason I do not tell her ahead of time that we are going for a walk and then whip her into her carrying case for a jaunt to Kim, the vet, for a check-up. I wait until I can pick her up casually without saying anything. Then she understands this too and begins to squirm and make sobbing sounds.

But the communication between cats and those who belong to them (what cat owners do not?) goes beyond any words. The best argument for ESP is to have a cat. I may, for instance, be working at the typewriter and stop to think that I might fix the flounder fillet for Amber's supper. Amber is probably asleep on my lap or on the pile of manuscript paper on the desk, but instantly she is wide awake and skimming to the kitchen, where she sits on the counter by the refrigerator, waiting for service.

This, also, has nothing to do with time sense, since it is a random thought I may have at any moment. But random or not, I find myself getting the flounder out and putting it on to cook while Amber begins to purr and watch every movement. I resort to more pedestrian communication when I mash it up.

"It will be hot now. You'll have to let it cool."

Amber's pink tongue licks her chops, but she makes no move toward the fish until I test it with my forefinger and suggest that if she eats around the edges first, the dish will be cool enough. Then she takes a tentative bite and begins to eat.

Or sometimes I am sitting quietly reading and remember I have to go to a party before long. I look up to find Amber sitting on the sofa looking stricken. Her eyes are wide with disbelief. (Are you going to leave me alone again?) I begin explaining, but her mournful gaze never wavers, and when I finally get up to go, she jumps to the harvest table by the door and reaches out a pitiful paw toward me.

This reminds me, by the way, of the cheery souls who say it is easier to have a cat than a dog. Dogs bark and when they are puppies sometimes tear things up when they are left alone, whereas you can leave a cat any time. A cat doesn't care. I have no idea how this myth started.

My cats have all been miserable when they are on the wrong side of the door. Reason tells me that Amber, after she hears the car drive away, goes back to take a nap or toss pencils around.

But when I come back, the sight of that desolate small face pressed against the window screen makes me wonder if I couldn't have managed to stay home. The intensity of her gaze and the quiver of her mouth are evidence that she herself thinks it is pretty silly for us to be parted.

If a neighbor happens to drop in while I am gone, I am often told there was no sign of my kitten at all. Amber tells me, in her own way, that she couldn't care less who else comes and goes or how many cars drive up. She wants to hear a particular motor and a special voice.

Perhaps the most spectacular exhibition of ESP, to return to that, is of a cat named Percy who lives in an apartment house, nine stories up, and instantly senses when the owner comes in nine floors down and goes to the elevator. I do not argue about this.

There are many things we do not understand about the reasons for behavior of animals or mankind. I do not know why suddenly Amber feels she wants to get in a bureau drawer and jumps up and down trying to pry the drawer open until I give in. Once in, she pokes her face at me, smiling and purring. Does she want to get away from it all, as the saying goes? Or does she sense that a noisy truck is going to drive up and four large rolls of carpet will slide across the floor?

Why do we both one day feel tense and nervous, and ten minutes later a sonic boom shakes the house until every picture on the walls is crooked? Sometimes on a cloudy day Amber begins to pace restlessly, back and forth, forth and back. I now know enough to shut all the windows just in time before a thunderstorm descends with no warning.

When Amber stands on tiptoe at the front door, peering through the screen, I hurry to brush my hair and put on some lipstick before that unexpected carload of guests arrive!

Nobody needs radar if there is a cat around!

Amber is very sensitive as to how I feel. If I am depressed after reading of one more tragic "incident" in the world, she gives up her own pursuits and runs to me to rub her cheek against my face and obviously try to comfort me. When I lost a very special friend in an automobile accident, she simply glued herself to me, looking at me with saucer eyes and purring in a different register from the usual happy one.

And when I broke my wrist, she was obviously more upset than I was—with the result I had to be gay, no matter how frustrated I was. It was actually good therapy. Her expression as she sat watching me try to brush my hair with my left hand holding the brush always made me laugh.

One friend reports that her cat "tried like crazy to be a nurse" when someone was ill in the household.

The attitude toward death is the same with most cats. When one friend of mine died, the family cat simply disappeared for two days and was finally located huddling under the bushes, wet, hungry, bedraggled. This same beautiful gray cat vanished when seriously injured, obviously feeling he should retire to die alone.

W. H. Hudson the naturalist, who loved cats, said, "Cats are mentally near to us, their brains function even as ours do." I feel this reaction to the inescapable fact of death is shared by animals and humankind, for most of us have an urge to go away from it as if, perhaps, that might make death go away and things be again as they should be. I also know a good many people who want to shut themselves away when they are ill. "Just let me alone," one of them says. Another remarks, "I don't want anybody around bothering me."

Both cats and we ourselves are unable to make peace with death and react in much the same way, denying it as best we can.

Chapter 15

Amber is now fully grown, although strangers always say with admiration, "What a beautiful kitten!" She will always be small and slight, probably never weighing as much as six pounds. But her coat has a deeper apricot tone so that at times it seems almost to give out light. The narrow wedge of her face has changed subtly so that she looks mature: looks more solid and her eyes seem even bigger. She has finally gained enough weight so the ribcage is fairly well upholstered. Her paws are bigger and the pads are like black raspberries. Her tail is no longer a quivering string but a firm length of seal brown.

In any situation now she stands on her own feet. If something upsets her, she firms into a tight ball and hisses fiercely. She is less apt to retreat from anything frightening. Her curiosity has increased, if possible. Her nose pokes into everything that comes into the house, from grocery bags and cartons to laundry packages.

She now comes when called, no matter how busy she is or how sound asleep. I did not train her to do this.

When I called her in the beginning and she came, I assumed it was an accident. I had planned to use the routine for dogs, which is to give a tidbit and much praise when they come, until the pattern is established; I would begin with her harness on, pull it lightly as I called, then give the reward. But I never got around to it, and suddenly I discovered she had trained herself. I can stand in the middle of the living room any time of day or night and call her and she comes dashing to me from the wing (on the Cape) or the back kitchen at Stillmeadow. She never looks for a tidbit. She is the only cat I have ever had who invariably would come when called, just as my cockers and Irish always have.

Perhaps this is not unusual, but it is in my experience. I may go all through the house looking to see where she is and there is no sign of her small person. Then I call "Amber! Amber!" and she materializes from some secret nook.

This past summer was the hottest in my area since records had been kept. This may have been the reason my nonshedding cat began to shed fluffs of apricot fur, giving me a chance to study individual hairs. Each has about two thirds of the glowing apricot color (the fanciers call it ruddy). Toward the tip is a pin point of grayish white. The top is a rich seal brown like her tail. This type of coloring is called ticking, although I have no idea why. In any case, the effect is luminous with the apricot shining through, accented by the ticking.

The shedding made the following typical:

"Yes, I do love you, but let me finish my grapefruit and coffee. Then I'll brush you."

Amber sits by the tray looking at me.

"It won't take me long, but I do want to finish my breakfast."

Amber looks at me.

"Amber, I wait on you day and night, but I do have to make a decision now and then. You go and eat your own breakfast."

Amber looks at me.

I put down the tray and go for the brush.

The purring begins and increases in volume as I brush and brush and brush. Cold coffee isn't too bad, considering. And after all, she only gets brushed five times a day!

I begin to worry about the barn cats in Connecticut. Perhaps they run through enough brush while hunting to lose some excess hair, or roll in the grass. I am sure nobody gives them sweet butter or oil to help prevent hair balls. If I put it out, it is a treat for ants and other insects.

The cooler days of fall stop the shedding, fortunately, and Amber's coat is satiny again.

One new achievement for Amber this season is figuring out how doors work. Luckily the doorknobs at Stillmeadow and on the Cape are so hard to turn that it takes both of my hands to manage them. After which I kick the door open.

I came in one day to find Amber swinging desperately on the living room doorknob, trying to make it turn with both front paws. She braced her hind paws on the door itself, which has a slight molding. Her tail was balancing the act by switching from side to side.

Another time the door was ajar and she was standing

bolt upright trying to push it open with her nose. She had one paw in the narrow opening and used it to pry.

Some of the doors in the 1690 house have the old hand-wrought latches. Amber tried to solve this by leaping in the air and landing with all five pounds on the latch. She did not get the latch up, but accomplished her purpose because I stopped working and took her out for a walk.

If a window is not raised high enough for her to sharpen her claws on the screen, she makes herself into a ball and heaves on the sash with all her strength. This also works, because I open the window until there is room enough for her to make extra holes in the screen.

She really enjoys having Kim manicure her claws and when we get home spreads her paws happily and polishes them off. If I am too slow getting her to Kim, she sits on my lap and tries to clip the tips herself. This results in my making a phone call, getting out her carrying case and starting off.

If she could run on the beach on the Cape, she would never need a manicure, but I would be minus a kitten. I admire the freedom my neighbor's cats enjoy—Smutzie and Tinker can roam at will; they weigh three times as much as Amber and really are more than a match for any wandering dog or coon. Often, however, when the family is ready to go back to Brockton after a week end, the cats are just not around! In that case, the family sits down and waits until the cats are ready to come in.

One habit that has grown on Amber is the desire to drink only water from the faucet. This is the same water that comes from the well and with which I fill her clean water dish. But when she is thirsty, she goes to the sink and sits, looking steadfastly at the faucet. I have to turn it on just enough to produce a small drip. Delicately she tiptoes toward it and turns her head to one side and drinks as the drops fall. An outside observer would comment on how mistreated my kitten is —not even a drink of water for her! But this just tastes better.

This summer her interest in television widened from watching the weatherman who uses a pointer to Johnny Cash, the country singer. She sits, spellbound, with wide dreamy eyes. I am also an addict of this remarkable performer, and I am sure my eyes have the same look as hers. I do not know whether it is the movement of his hands on the guitar or the sound itself which enraptures her, but in any case Amber is a Johnny Cash fan, and I imagine this might surprise him.

During most musical hours, she dozes, or scrubs herself, or chases an errant moth.

We have, on Cape Cod, what we call sour bugs which get in the house somehow during damp weather. They are small oval grayish bugs that just appear and wander around aimlessly. They never seem to eat anything or to have any purpose; they just move across the rug or crawl up a wall. Amber's reaction to them is strange considering that she is so excited about a moth or ant or fly. She tiptoes past them, not even putting out a tentative paw to examine them. Perhaps they do have a strange smell. But anything else that moves catches her attention instantly.

I happen to have a phobia about these bugs and cannot ignore them, and it seems to me I never sit down to relax but that one small bug appears on the beige rug, just going back and forth. Amber never helps me dispose of one. As she watches me scoop the creature up with a tissue, her gaze is fathomless.

The people who say a cat has no expression have obviously never lived with one. Amber has no trouble expressing any emotion she feels, and all without raising a paw. Her whiskers quiver with excitement, her eyes widen and her shell-pink ears prick forward when something surprises her. When she is melancholy, she can look like Niobe. When she is pleased, she smiles. She flexes her lips and has a beaming look. The purr throbs in her throat at the same time, and if she is ecstatic, she spreads her paws. But the smile comes first.

Amber seldom gets angry, but when she does, she reminds me of a small jungle tiger. Her whiskers flatten, her ears vibrate, her pupils dilate, and she reinforces this with a sharp hiss from between clenched teeth. She never hisses at me, but sometimes with others she seems to have a dire need to defend her personality. I am divided between feeling apologetic because she has lost her temper and being thankful she is not too passive! Which shows what contradictory creatures we all are.

Only a cat lover would understand that when Amber looks wistful I melt like a candle in hot sun. She reminds me of the lily maid of Astolat. She bends her head slightly, her golden lashes droop, the corners of her mouth curve downward, her ears are straight. I may have been at the typewriter too long, or there may be a rabbit outside the window she wants to chase, or she may feel it is time for some bits of steak. It is my business to find out. I always manage to.

Amber has developed one gift which is unusual, in my experience. When I suggest a walk, she levitates to the harvest table, quivering with excitement. She holds her head forward so I can slip the collar piece on. The strap is comfortable for I use the same recipe as for collars on a dog. If I can slip two fingers between the leather and her chest, it is loose enough but still safe. But when I fasten the strap, she is in a hurry. She manages to utter a squeak and purr at the same time. Her message is plain. I am slow and fumbling, which I am, but she loves the idea of going out so she would not want me to give up trying to get the small fastener closed.

I would like to suggest to the manufacturers a harness that fastens on the top instead of under the stomach, or even on the side. I have to hold up her left leg and at the same time bend double to see the tiny hole the strap goes in.

I was thinking as we took our walk today, and while she chose just the particular grass tip she wanted to nibble, that all of us, in some way, are subjected to harnesses, but if they offer safety and security we should be grateful. Certainly Amber adores hers.

I also wished we could adjust as gracefully to the end of something as Amber does. She would like to stay out indefinitely, tiptoeing around or lunging at the yard rabbit, but when we have to go indoors, she follows me and waits for me to open the door. Then she trots in and stands while I unfasten the harness.

When I go back to the typewriter, she bounces onto my lap, suggesting that I should spend my time holding her and appreciating how wonderful she is! I am reminded of a friend who once said she never would have a cocker because they are too affectionate. I would never advise an Abyssinian for such a person.

Amber and I are satisfied with each other. We like to share everything. And I do not find anything so important that I cannot stop it while I hold her against my cheek and tell her for the millionth time that she is the most beautiful and best. Nor is she ever too involved with a dish of minced steak to forget me. She stops and makes her air-borne way from the counter to my lap. She gives me a few sandpapery kisses, and then goes back to finish off her steak.

And when I am ready for sleep at night, she sits on the foot of the bed, waiting for me to say, "Amber, I love you," before she folds herself into a furry ball and purrs herself to sleep.

Amber, I love you.